Stuart Barlow is in the family team at Bhatia Best Solicitors. He has specialised in Family Law for over 40 years. His focus is now on representing Parents and other parties in Children Cases. He is a member of the Law Society Children Panel and Accredited Specialist with Resolution in Private Children and Cohabitation Law. He is the former Chief Assessor of the Law Society Family Law Panel and adjudicator for the Legal Aid Agency. He is a regular presenter of training courses for family lawyers throughout England and Wales and the author of several family law books.

A Practical Guide to the Rights of Grandparents in Children Proceedings

Second Edition

A Practical Guide to the Rights of Grandparents in Children Proceedings

Second Edition

Stuart Barlow

LLB (London) Solicitor

Law Brief Publishing

Published 2023 by Law Brief Publishing, an imprint of Law Brief Publishing Ltd
30 The Parks
Minehead
Somerset
TA24 8BT

www.lawbriefpublishing.com

Paperback: 978-1-914608-91-9

This book is dedicated to my wonderful wife, Sue, the devoted Grandma of our six grandchildren: Bethany, Sam, Joseph, Rosie, Ava and Flynn.

PREFACE

I first began to think seriously about the rights of grandparents during a court case in the Cardiff County Court in 1979. I was representing a mother who was opposing her husband's application for an order to see his daughter. During cross examination my client was asked by the father's advocate why she opposed the order. She responded:

"My husband has no interest in seeing our daughter."

"But he is applying for an order. Why is that?" asked the advocate.

My client replied: "Because he only wants the order so that his parents can see her. He is not bothered."

The mother was objecting because the proposed order was for the grandparents' benefit and not the father's.

The Judge hearing the case, intervened by asking my client: "So, do you not think it is a good thing for grandparents to see their grandchildren?" There was only silence from my client as she realised the impact of the Judge's question.

Ever since that occasion, I have often thought about how family conflict impacts the lives of grandparents and what limited rights they have in maintaining what is often a close and loving relationship with their grandchildren. The law does not always give grandparents a high priority in the lives of their grandchildren, especially in private law proceedings.

I would like to give special thanks to my wife, Sue, who is also grandmother to our six grandchildren. She has encouraged me in the writing and editing of this book.

I also thank the publishers, Law Brief Publishing, who suggested the idea of the book and have supported and encouraged me.

The contents of the book as to law and procedure are correct as at 20th March 2023.

I hope this book is accessible, not only to professional advisers, but also to anyone who seeks to help grandparents and to grandparents themselves.

Stuart Barlow
March 2023

CONTENTS

INTRODUCTION

Many grandparents have in recent times acquired an increasingly important role in the lives of their grandchildren. Changes in family life have meant that grandparents frequently care for their grandchildren in roles ranging from occasional babysitting and the school run to having almost full-time care.

In the case of Social Services intervention, where parents are not able to care for their children, grandparents step into a surrogate role in order to avoid the children being cared for outside the family. The resulting close bond that can develop between grandparent and grandchild might then be under threat when parents separate or family conflict arises and the grandparent can suddenly feel helpless and alone.

Grandparents will often seek advice on how that relationship can be restored, possibly by judicial or similar intervention. I have become increasingly aware that the material available to those advising grandparents within private and public proceedings is sketchy and only to be found within wider family law publications.

The purpose of this book is to bring together a source of information in one place for all those called upon to advise grandparents facing such situations.

CHAPTER ONE

SUMMARY OF THE CURRENT POSITION

1. The Children Act 1989 (even in its amended form) makes no specific reference to grandparents. They have no immediate superior role to other family members.

2. Successive governments have considered whether grandparents should be given the facility to apply for a section 8 order in their own right and have decided this is not appropriate; **The Family Justice Review Report 2011** at paragraph 4.41-4.48 concluded that notwithstanding the importance of grandparents, the requirement for them to seek leave should remain. This is still the position.

3. Most cases require a grandparent to make an initial application **for permission** to file a section 8 application-which creates a two-stage process;

4. There are some situations where a grandparent can make an immediate application, but these are limited;

5. The reasoning behind the **two-stage process** is to filter out inappropriate applications as a protection against interference in the child's care, comfort, and security;

6. Any application by a grandparent for permission is unlikely to succeed if a similar application is being made by another party.

For example, when a father is making an application for an order to see his children, and his own parents (the grandparents) want to see the children at a different time. The court is likely to see the grandparents' own application as a duplication of the father's application, as there is no reason why the children cannot see the grandparents at the same time as their father. **Re W (A child) (Care Proceedings: Leave to Apply) 2005 2 FLR 468**

7. Special Guardianship Orders have received some scrutiny by the courts and the government in recent years and changes are slowly taking place to update this important area of family law

CHAPTER TWO

COMMON SITUATIONS FACED BY GRANDPARENTS

1. **The need to acquire Parental Responsibility**. This is where there is a need to acquire parental responsibility. It could be that the grandchild has been living with the grandparent for some time and and the grandparent feels powerless to make important decisions on behalf of the child. For example, there has been a visit to a hospital and the hospital has queried the grandparents right to make a decision for the grandchild; **In B v B (A Minor) (Residence order [1992] 2 FLR 327** a grandmother applied to the Magistrates Court for a residence order in respect of her granddaughter who had lived with her for some time to enable her to have parental responsibility. Her application was supported by the mother. The application was refused on the "no order principle", Section 1(5) Children Act 1989. This decision was overturned on appeal stating that a residence order should be granted where there was a need to acquire parental responsibility.

2. **When Parents Divorce or Separate. This is** where the parents separate and the grandparent has been refused any contact with the grandchild or for some other reason they lose contact with them. Research has shown that when parents separate around 42 per cent of grandparents lose contact with their grandchildren.

3. **When the parents refuse the grandparent any contact with their children.** It could be there has been a falling-out between the adults within the family, and the grandchildren are caught up in the dispute. The end result is that the parents refuse the grandparent any ongoing relationship with their children.

4. **Involvement of Social Services.** This is when an application comes before the court as a result of Social Services becoming involved with the family. The parents may be unable to care for their children safely and Social Services look to the grandparents to care for the children, maybe in the short term or even long term.

Grandparents and relatives

Grandparents and other relatives may make court applications regarding their grandchildren. Grandparents applying for contact is common. Applications for other orders e.g. to enable the grandchild to reside with the grandparent will also arise from time to time.

Thorpe J in **Re J (Leave to issue application for residence order (2003) 1 FLR 114** suggested that trial judges should recognise the greater appreciation that has developed of the value of what grandparents have to offer their grandchildren, particularly those who have disabled parents.

Informal Arrangements

Informal care arrangements can often take place where relatives look after a child but they have no parental responsibility and the child is not a 'looked after' child by the Local Authority. Informal arrangements are made between the parent of the child and the relative concerned in caring for the child. Sometimes there is no clear agreement and the terms of placement are undefined. As the carer has no parental responsibility for the child in question, the carer is powerless in making major decisions, such as medical treatment, schooling and travel abroad. Parents can end the arrangement at any time and without notice. Grandparents can be put in this position and have no immediate recourse to any principle in law. The grandparent may wish to apply to the court for an order that would give them parental responsibility and at the same time confirm the residence position for the child.

CHAPTER THREE

ORDERS AVAILABLE TO GRANDPARENTS

Child Arrangements Order Section 8 Children Act 1989 {as amended)

A Child Arrangements Order confirms where a child will live and with whom, and when he or she will spend time with a person or people other than those the child normally lives with. This is usually the parent, although can include grandparents and other relatives.

The Court will make a Child Arrangements Order if parents are unable to agree on the arrangements for where a child lives and spends time with a non-resident parent. A Child Arrangements Order can deal with:-

- which parent the child will live with;
- how much time the child will spend with the other parent (if any);
- when a child will spend time with the other parent;
- whether Contact with the other parent should be supervised.

An arrangement called **Shared Care** is becoming increasingly popular. It can provide for a child to live with both parents and spell out (within the CAO) how the time will be divided. A shared care arrangement can be made even if the division of time is unequal between the two homes.

Similar orders can be made in favour of the grandparent provided they have the court's permission to seek such an order or are exempt from doing so.

The terminology of the Children Act 1989 has changed over the years. Old expressions such as "Custody" and "Access" are often used, even though the terms disappeared many years ago. These were succeeded by the terms "Residence" and "Contact" which are no longer in existence. Orders made under the previous rules, will of course still exist.

Prohibited Steps Order Section 8 Children Act 1989

A Prohibited Steps Order (PSO) is an Order that forbids someone from exercising his or her powers of parental responsibility in a particular manner.

PSOs can cover many areas. Some of the more common examples of PSOs include forbidding a parent or grandparent to:-

- remove the child from the UK;
- change the child's name or allow him or her to be known by another name;
- change the child's school; and
- take the child for identified medical treatment.

PSOs may be made against any person (not just a child's parent): a PSO could be made against a family member or friend who it is feared might make a decision of a type usually taken by someone with PR.

Specific Issue Order, Section 8 Children Act 1989

A Specific Issue Order (SIO) is made where a dispute arises about a question of Parental Responsibility. The disagreement facing the Court dealing with an SIO is usually narrow and well-defined.

Examples of matters that might be the basis of an SIO include:-

1. which school a child should attend;
2. whether a child should have a particular course of treatment (such as a vaccination or operation);
3. in which religious rights the child should participate (for example circumcision; confirmation); and
4. whether the child should temporarily leave the UK for a holiday.

The Court will be asked to grant permission for a particular course of action i.e. a dispute between the parents or others with PR.

Child Arrangements Orders, PSOs and SIOs are sometimes referred to as **Section 8 Orders.** This is because the Court's power to make them comes from Section 8 of the Children Act 1989.

Most parents are entitled, as of right, to apply for a Section 8 Order relating to their children. Other family members and significant people in a child's life might also be able to apply for a Section 8 Order as of right. Those who cannot, need to ask the Court for permission to make the Application.

Section 8 Orders, once made, usually last until the child concerned reaches 16. In exceptional circumstances, an Order can last until the child reaches 18.

When considering whether to make a Section 8 Order, **the Court's first and overriding obligation is to the welfare of the child.**

The Court is required to have regard to a number of matters known as the **Welfare Checklist.**

The Court will proceed on the basis that **delay** in resolving a dispute about Section 8 Orders is **likely to prejudice** the welfare of the child.

The Court will not make a Section 8 Order unless it considers that doing so would be better for the child than making no order at all. This is called the "No Order" principle.

Appointment or Removal of a Guardian, Section 5 Children Act 1989

The Children Act 1989 introduces a concept of a child's **Guardian.** A Guardian is a person who assumes responsibility for, and has parental responsibility for a child on the death of his or her parents.

A parent with Parental Responsibility may appoint a Guardian in writing. This is often done in a will. The appointment only takes effect once all parents with PR for the child have died.

The Court also has the power to appoint a Guardian if there is no adult with PR for the child. The Court will take into account the same matters in deciding a question about Guardianship as it does when dealing with Section 8 Orders.

Special Guardianship Order, Section 115 Adoption and Children Act 2002

A Special Guardianship Order appoints one or more people as **Special Guardians** of the child. The Order lasts until the child is 18 unless it is changed by way of Court Order before then. The Special Guardian has parental responsibility for the child and can take most decisions about the child (such as where the child will live or go to school) without having to consult anyone else. The Special Guardian cannot change the child's surname or take the child abroad for more than three months without the agreement of anyone else with parental responsibility or the permission of the Court.

A Special Guardianship Order will enable the child to keep ties with his or her birth family, although the family's rights and responsibilities are reduced.

This type of order is commonly made in favour of a grandparent.

Adoption Order, Adoption and Children Act 2002

When the child is adopted, he or she becomes part of a "new" adoptive family and all legal ties with their birth family are cut. The birth parents lose their parental responsibility and the adoption order cannot, except on extremely rare occasions, be varied or discharged. Adoption by family members is rare, as an adoption order breaks the link between the child and the birth parent and transfers parental responsibility to the adopters. However, some adoptions are "open", in that the child remains in contact with the birth parents. Grandparents may find themselves in this position.

Order for Financial Provision for a Child

Financial support for a child will usually be by reference to the **Child Maintenance Services** (CMS) who will calculate a level of child support payable by an absent parent by way of a formula applicable to most parents. The main carer for the child can make an application. This will include the grandparent.

There are some situations where the CMS will not be able to assist, or where the formula may be less helpful. These include the following:-

- some families where either the parents or the child ordinarily live outside of the UK;
- if the paying parents net income is more than £104,000 per annum;
- where a child has special needs; and
- where a child is beyond secondary education.

In these situations, the Court retains the ability to look at what level of regular financial support is suitable. This is under **Schedule 1 of the Children Act 1989.** The Court will be guided by, but not bound by, the CMS formulas.

Beyond the question of regular financial support, there are other types of financial provision to benefit a child that a Court is able to Order under Section 1. One very common example is where there is a dispute about parents' contributions towards school fees. Private school fees are not dealt with by the CMS and an application to court would need to be made if there were any disagreements about who ought to pay.

The Court will take into account all the family circumstances.

Under Schedule 1, the definition of a child's "parent" is wider than normal. It includes a child's biological mother and father but also any other person to whom they are or were married, so long as the child was 'treated as a child of the family'. An application under Section 1 might be made against a step-parent or former step-parent.

Who can apply for a financial order?

1. A claim for financial provision on behalf of a child can be made by a parent, guardian or special guardian of a child, or by any person who is named in a child arrangements order as a person with whom a child is to live (**para 1(1) Sch 1**).

2. A child is defined in **S.105(1) CA 1989** as a person under the age of eighteen.

3. The child must live with the applicant: **N v C (Financial Provision; Schedule 1 Claims Dismissed)** [2013] EWHC 399(Fam).

What orders are available?

If the applicant is acting in a parental capacity and the application is on behalf a child, he or she can apply for one or more of the following orders:

- Secured periodical payments (for themselves on the child's behalf or to the child himself) – **para 1(2)(b) Sch1;**

- Lump sum (for themselves on the child's behalf or to the child himself) – **para 1(2)(c) Sch1;**

- Settlement of property for the benefit of the child – **para 1(2)(d) Sch1;**
- Transfer of property (to applicant on the child's behalf or to the child himself) – **para 1(2)(e) Sch1.**

CHAPTER FOUR

WHO CAN APPLY? – SECTION 10 CHILDREN ACT 1989

Who Can Apply? Section 10 Children Act 1989

Section 10 of the Children Act 1989 states:

> ***Power of court to make section 8 orders.***
>
> *(1) In any family proceedings in which a question arises with respect to the welfare of any child, the court may make a section 8 order with respect to the child if—*
>
> *(a) an application for the order has been made by a person who—*
>
> *(i) is entitled to apply for a section 8 order with respect to the child; or*
>
> *(ii) has obtained the leave of the court to make the application; or*
>
> *(b) the court considers that the order should be made even though no such application has been made.*
>
> *(2) The court may also make a section 8 order with respect to any child on the application of a person who—*

(a) is entitled to apply for a section 8 order with respect to the child; or

(b) has obtained the leave of the court to make the application.

(3) This section is subject to the restrictions imposed by section 9.

(4) The following persons are entitled to apply to the court for any section 8 order with respect to a child—

(a) any parent guardian or special guardian of the child;

(aa) any person who by virtue of section 4A has parental responsibility for the child;

(b) any person who is named, in a child arrangements order that is in force with respect to the child, as a person with whom the child is to live.

(5) The following persons are entitled to apply for a child arrangements order with respect to a child—

(a) any party to a marriage (whether or not subsisting) in relation to whom the child is a child of the family;

(aa) any civil partner in a civil partnership (whether or not subsisting) in relation to whom the child is a child of the family;

(b) any person with whom the child has lived for a period of at least three years;

(c) any person who—

(i) in any case where a child arrangements order in force with respect to the child regulates arrangements relating

to with whom the child is to live or when the child is to live with any person, has the consent of each of the persons named in the order as a person with whom the child is to live;

(ii) in any case where the child is in the care of a local authority, has the consent of that authority; or

(iii) in any other case, has the consent of each of those (if any) who have parental responsibility for the child.

(d) any person who has parental responsibility for the child by virtue of provision made under section 12(2A).

(5A) A local authority foster parent is entitled to apply for a child arrangements order to which subsection (5C) applies with respect to a child if the child has lived with him for a period of at least one year immediately preceding the application.

(5B) A relative of a child is entitled to apply for a child arrangements order to which subsection (5C) applies with respect to the child if the child has lived with the relative for a period of at least one year immediately preceding the application.

(5C) This subsection applies to a child arrangements order if the arrangements regulated by the order relate only to either or both of the following—

(a) with whom the child concerned is to live, and

(b) when the child is to live with any person.

Summary

There are a number of situations when the grandparent **is not** obliged to seek the court's permission to file a Section 8 application. They are:

1. If the child is in the care of the Local Authority and the Local Authority supports the application;
2. The applicant is a Guardian;
3. Where all the parties with Parental Responsibility consent to permission being granted;
4. The applicant is a Special Guardian;
5. When the applicant is named in a Child Arrangements Order providing for residence;
6. The applicant is a foster parent and the child has been living with him/her for one year or more;
7. A "relative" who has cared for the child for one year more; The definition of "a relative" is wide and clearly includes "any grandparent".

CHAPTER FIVE

WHAT IF THE COURT'S PERMISSION IS REQUIRED?

If a grandparent is seeking the courts' permission to file a Section 8 application, the authorities are found in the **Family Procedure Rules 2010 Part 18 and Practice Direction 2010 18A.**

The test for deciding an application for the grant of permission was addressed in **Re J (Leave to Issue Application For Residence Order (2003)1FLR 114** when the court stated that the statutory checklist in **Section 10(9)** must be given its proper recognition and weight. Applicants enjoy a right to a fair trial pursuant to **Article 6** and in the nature of things they very often enjoy Article 8 rights,

To support an application for leave the case **Re J (A Child) (Leave to issue application for Residence Order)** [2002] **EWCA Civ 1346** can be used as a precedent.

The mother was a psychiatric in-patient and the local authority wanted to place her 18-month-old daughter for adoption. An older child had largely been raised by the paternal grandparents and to a lesser extent by the maternal grandmother and was about to go to university.

The Local Authority had rejected the grandmother as a possible carer due to her volatile relationship with her daughter and her age, which was 59. It said the application did not merit judicial consideration. Nevertheless the grandmother applied to be joined as a party and for leave to apply for residence. The mother supported the application as had the father prior to the Local Authority's objection.

The lower court had not adequately considered the **Section 10(9)** checklist; the question for the Court was: 'Has the applicant satisfied the Court that he or she has a good arguable case for the criteria that Parliament applied in section 10(9)?' The Court allowed the application, accorded the grandmother party status and allowed her to make an application for residence.

Section 10 (9) of the Children Act 1989 sets out a short check list of **what the court will consider** when dealing with an **application for permission.**

These are:

1. The nature of the proposed order — in other words, what order is your client seeking;

2. The applicant's connection with the child—in our case, a grandparent;

3. Risk of disruption or harm to the child. If the child has been living with another adult, what the consequences are of any move for the child should your client's application be successful. Alternatively, if the child is already living with the grandparent, why the court should change this arrangement.

4. If the child is in the care of the Local Authority, what are their plans for the child?

5. The views of the parents, remembering that the parents have every right to be heard on the application;

It should be note that the caselaw has made it clear that the list in **Section 10 (9) is "not exhaustive".**

The words "**particular regard**" in **Section 10** (9) implies that there **may be** other factors for the court need to take into account when dealing with a **permission application.**

One example may be "**the prospects of success**" of the substantive applicant.

In the case of **Re B (Paternal Grandmother: Joinder as Party) 2012 2 FLR 1358** the court said the application **must be arguable** if permission to file is granted.

But even if it is arguable, there is no guarantee that the application for permission will **necessarily** be granted.

The court will, of course, take into account all the other factors.

One particular case of help when applying for permission to file a Section 8 application is:

Re A (A Child – Application for leave to apply for a child arrangements order) [2015] EWFC 47

The application concerned Alice, a 9-year old girl, whose family structure was of a complex nature. Alice was born to Rachel (her biological mother) and David (a known sperm donor who lived abroad and did not have parental responsibility). Rachel was in a civil partnership with Helen (her non-biological mother).

Both Rachel and Helen had mental health issues. (Rachel, schizophrenia and schizo-affective disorder and Helen, emotionally unstable personality disorder, anxiety and depression). Helen had limited mobility and received support from local authority carers. She also had two adult children from a previous relationship, one of whom (Susan) had physical and learning difficulties.

When they separated in 2009, Rachel was detained under the Mental Health Act 1983. Alice then went to live with Helen under a residence order (made by consent) where she had remained ever since. Following her discharge from hospital, Rachel has had supervised contact to Alice, provided for in the consent order.

Helen started a relationship with Matthew (a female to male transsexual in the process of transitioning, who also had mental health difficulties). The relationship subsisted from 2009 – 2013, during the course of which Matthew played a role in the care of Alice. When they separated, Matthew entered into his current relationship with James.

There were disputes as to fact, with Matthew and Helen each alleging abusive behaviour on the part of the other. Helen alleged that, due to Matthew's aggression caused by the testosterone used in his transitioning, they did not live together continuously and Matthew asserted that he had been in the "dominant parent role".

After their separation, Matthew continued to have contact to Alice for about 16 months, following which it ceased in acrimonious circumstances. Matthew then applied for leave to seek a child arrangements order.

Alice herself had been diagnosed with autism spectrum disorder. She was also said to have experienced some gender confusion, spending a period identifying as a boy.

David, with whom Alice had established a relationship by social media and occasional visits, was aware of the application and opposed it.

Rachel also opposed the application, considering that Alice's wellbeing had improved markedly since Matthew's departure.

Due to the exceptional circumstances, HHJ Bellamy made Alice a party and appointed a guardian. Her enquiries revealed that Alice had been subject to local authority involvement. Alice herself was reported to be aware of the proceedings but disinterested in the outcome.

If the application was to proceed, it would entail expert psychiatric evidence, disclosure of the local authority documents and a fact finding hearing.

Having set out s.10 Children Act 1989 in full, the judge noted that it was accepted that Matthew had to seek leave, pursuant to s.10(9).

He then considered the relevant case engineering, citing, in particular, Black LJ's comments in *Re B (A child)* [2012] EWCA Civ 737 to the effect that s.10(9) did not contain a test, merely factors to which the court should have regard. One of these factors was plainly the prospect of success, but simply having an arguable case would not necessarily be sufficient. Additionally, whilst the child's welfare was not paramount, it was still relevant.

In terms of Matthew's role, drawing on Baroness Hale's judgment in *Re G (Children) (Residence: Same-sex Partner)*[2006] UKHL 43, his claim to "parenthood" could only be as a "psychological" parent.

On his behalf it was asserted that his role in Alice's life both before and after the separation (said to be analogous to that of a step parent) and the "minimal impact" an order would have on her, militated in favour of leave being granted.

In addition, it was argued that he would have been able to apply as of right (by virtue of having lived with her for 3 years) had he applied earlier and that it would be unfair to prejudice his position because in seeking to avoid litigation he had not issued sooner.

Helen, although accepting that Alice was a child of the family, asserted that the impact of granting leave would be considerable and would bring her into a harmful arena of conflict.

The guardian felt that reintroduction of Matthew would have to be sustainable and of significant benefit to Alice, given the "extensive" number of adults with whom she was already involved.

Rachel asserted that granting the application would exacerbate Helen's health issues to Alice's detriment and might restart her gender confusion. She did not need a father-figure as she had two mothers. Moreover, Matthew's own mental health issues were ongoing.

The guardian noted Matthew had been a significant adult and could potentially be a father figure but also the risk of Helen's health deteriorating to Alice's detriment.

In considering the application, HHJ Bellamy looked at the s.10(9) factors in the light of the authorities, noting that, although he was not making a finding, the evidence strongly suggested that, in relation to the "connection with the child" required by s.10(9)(b), Matthew had become a psychological parent.

With respect to whether or not such a relationship could also be lost over time, s.10(5)(b) provided that the right to make an application based on 3 years of living with the child, expired after 3 months had elapsed. If granted, the court would need to determine not only if Matthew had been a psychological parent but also, if he had ceased to be so.

With regard to the issue of risk of disruption to the child (s.10(9) (c)) given the features of Helen's illnesses, combined with her older daughter's needs and Alice's autism, this family had considerable care needs and would find continued litigation burdensome and disruptive. Accordingly, HHJ Bellamy concluded that there was a risk of the application causing harm to Alice.

The risk element had to be balanced with other factors and the court had to take account of all elements of the case. In this instance, the extensive range of adult relationships available to Alice was relevant.

As for whether or not Matthew had an arguable case, although there were positive factors to weigh in the balance, those on the other side included the range of adults with whom Alice was already engaged, the health needs of those adults and her own autism. On balance, the judge was satisfied that the case was, at best "barely arguable".

Accordingly, taking a global view, the application should be refused.

CHAPTER SIX

OTHER IMPORTANT FACTORS

The Welfare Test

In **Section 8** applications, **"the welfare of the children test"** always applies.

However, this does not apply at **the permission stage.**

Otherwise known as the "paramountcy test" (**Section 1(1) Children Act 1989** it was held in **Re A (Minors) (Residence Orders: Leave to Apply) (1992) 3 All ER 872** that the welfare of the child is not the courts paramount consideration **when determining whether or not to grant leave to apply**. In granting or refusing an application for leave to apply for a section 8 application, the court is not determining a question with respect to the upbringing of the child concerned. The question only arises when the court hears the substantive application. It will, however, be a factor, but not a **determining** factor.

G v Kirklees MBC (1993) 1FLR 505 confirms this decision.

Human Rights

All grandparent applications for permission will be taken seriously by the courts.

Articles 6 & 8 of the European Convention of Human Rights give grandparents the right to a **fair trial** and **respect for family life.**

Whatever the nature of any application by a grandparent, the court is **under a duty** to give it careful attention.

In the case of **Re J (Leave to issue application for residence order) 2002 EWCA Civ 1346** the court held that the minimal essential protection of a grandparent's human rights was that their application should not be dismissed without **full enquiry.**

In the later case of **Re B (Paternal Grandmother: Joinder as Party) (2012) 2FLR 1358 at paragraph 51** "full enquiry" must be read in the context of the facts of the particular case being dealt with.

What about the age of the grandparent?

A feature that often arises in grandparent cases is the question of age.

It is sometimes argued that the grandparent is too old to care for a child. This subject is not specifically mentioned in the **Section10 (9)** check list but will be a factor the court will take into account when deciding whether permission should be granted when dealing with the grandparent's application.

In the case of **Re C (A Child) (2009) EWCA Civ 72** the Court of Appeal warned lower courts against making assumptions that grandparents cannot provide proper care because of their old age. The court made it clear that whilst age will be a factor, it is not necessarily an overriding factor.

In this case, the child's mother and father were separated and had drug problems which meant that it was very unlikely that either would be able to provide a home for the child or his older half-sister. The two children were currently in short term foster care and the local authority's plan was to leave the older child in foster care while seeking adoption for the younger child. The guardian supported that plan but the paternal grandmother was joined into the proceedings and sought a residence order supported by all the other parties, including the half-sister. The trial judge dismissed the local authority's application for care and placement orders and made a residence order instead.

The local authority appealed on the grounds that the judge's conclusion was plainly wrong on the primary basis that it was wrong to leave the proceedings on the basis that "the family will rally round if and when the grandmother's circumstances disable her from continuing to act as his primary carer". However Wilson LJ, while accepting that the circumstances were unusual, dismissed the appeal because i) the residence order was in favour of a member of the child's wider family, and the law is biased in favour of such placements; ii) most importantly, the grandmother had a good relationship and substantial track-record of commitment to the child in very difficult circumstances; iii) the grandmother was sincere in expressing commitment to the idea of substantial continuing contact between the child and his half-sister.

Lord Justice Wilson stated: 'Fundamentally, this appeal turns upon the age of the grandmother and the likelihood that, irrespective of whether she remains alive for the next thirteen years, she will prove incapable, at any rate towards the end of that period, of caring satisfactorily for J.'

Summary of the Law on Permission

The case of **Re A (2015) All ER (D) 24** gives a **helpful summary** of what the court is looking for when deciding **on a permission application:**

1. Every case is **fact specific**;
2. **Section 10(9)** sets out a check list but is "not exhaustive";
3. All material facts will be taken into account including whether there is an arguable case;
4. The welfare of the child is **relevant** but **not a paramount consideration.**

Should the court **refuse** a party permission to file an application, there is a duty on the court to give reasons for that decision as stated in the case of **T v W (Contact Reasons) 1996 2 FLR 47**.

CHAPTER SEVEN

APPLICATION FOR PARTY STATUS

This is a subject that will arise when there are already court proceedings in relation to a child and a family member eg a grandparent seeks be involved in those proceedings. In addition, the grandparent may wish to apply for a court order. The grandparent will need to apply for party status. If party status is granted, they are entitled to attend future court hearings, have legal representation and have sight of all court papers. The court will consider the application for party status on its merits.

Re B (A child) [2012] EWCA Civ 737 concerned an application by a grandmother for joinder as a party to care proceedings. The leading judgment was given by Black LJ. It is clear from her judgment that the approach to a joinder application is similar to the approach to an application for leave under s.10. The following passages from the judgment bear on the decision made:

> '36. There is no guidance in the Children Act 1989 or the Family Procedure Rules 2010 which specifically assists as to the approach that should be taken to an application for joinder and the welfare of the child is not the paramount consideration in either an application for party status or an application for leave to make a substantive application because neither of these applications involves the court in determining "any question with respect to....the upbringing of a child"...

39. ...section 10(9) does not contain anything in the nature of a test by which an application should be judged, nor even criteria which must be satisfied before leave can be given, nor is anything of the kind to be derived from the rest of section 10. Neither does the subsection circumscribe the factors that can be taken into account in determining the leave application; it leaves the court to take into account all the material features of the case and merely highlights certain matters which are of particular relevance...

48. ...I do not see section 10(9) as containing a test. By picking out some factors to which the court should have "particular regard", it acknowledges by implication that there may be other factors which the court has to consider. It would be wrong, in my view, to try to list or limit these factors which will vary infinitely from case to case. One amongst them is plainly the prospects of success of the application that is proposed; leave will not be given for an application that is not arguable. I do not intend to attempt a definition of what is arguable but I would make a few observations before I leave the question of the proper approach to an application to which section 10(9) applies, whether directly or through an application to be joined as a party with a view to seeking the sort of outcome that could be the subject of a section 8 order.

49. The first observation is that the fact that a person has an arguable case may not necessarily be sufficient to entitle him or her to leave under section 10 or to joinder as a party. I say this because section 10(9) picks out other factors as requiring particular regard and I think it must follow that there may be situations in which, when the judge exercises his or her discretion, balancing all the relevant factors, the presence of an arguable case is outweighed by those other factors or, indeed, by any other factor that carries particular weight in the individual

circumstances of the case. Suppose, for example, that the applicant wishes to advance a barely arguable case with many attendant problems in relation to a child with special needs who is securely placed with an irreplaceable long term family who will be unable to withstand the rigours of any further litigation.

> 50. The second observation is that there is room, in cases concerning children, for applications or proposed applications to be checked at a very early stage and without wholesale investigation. The court has a broad discretion to conduct the case as is most appropriate given the issues involved and the evidence available, see for example *Re B (Minors((Contact)* [1994] 2 FLR 1, *Re C (Contact: Conduct of Hearings)* [2006] 2 FLR 289 and ***Re N; A v G and N*** **[2009] EWHC 1807 (Fam)**...'

As Black LJ noted, an application for leave under s.10 does not involve the court in determining 'any question with respect to...the upbringing of a child' for the purpose of s.1 of the Children Act 1989. It follows, therefore, that in determining Matthew's application Alice's welfare is not the court's paramount consideration. However, that does not mean that her welfare is of no relevance. In ***Warwickshire County Council v M*** **[2007] EWCA Civ 1084**, Wilson LJ (as he then was) said that

> '26. Whenever it is invested with a discretion whether to grant leave for proceedings to be issued, a court will have regard to the applicant's prospect of success in the proposed proceedings. From the sphere of proceedings relating to children I offer five examples:
>
> ...(c) An application under s.10(9) of the Act of 1989 for leave to apply for an order under s.8 requires the court to consider – in addition to other specified factors – "whether there is an

> arguable case": *G v. F (Contact and Shared Residence: Applications for Leave)* [1998] 2 FLR 799.'

He went on to make the point that,

> '29. In relation to an application for leave under s.24(3) of the [Adoption and Children Act 2002] I therefore hold that, on establishment of a change in circumstances, a discretion arises in which the welfare of the child and the prospect of success should both be weighed. My view is that the requisite analysis of the prospect of success will almost always include the requisite analysis of the welfare of the child...'

Variation or Discharge of a Section 8 Order

A person who is not otherwise entitled to apply for a variation or discharge of a Section 8 order shall be entitled to do so under **Section 10(6)** if:

1. The order was made on his application;

2. In the case of a Child Arrangements Order, he is named in the order as the person with whom the child concerned is to spend time or otherwise have contact with any person. This means that a child named in the Child Arrangements Order for which he had applied will not need leave to apply to vary it per Wilson J in **Re W (Application of Leave: Whether Necessary) 1996 Fam Law 665.** For this purpose no distinction is made between direct and indirect contact.

CHAPTER EIGHT

THE COURT PROCESS

Mediation

All applicants seeking a section 8 order will be required to attend a Mediation Information and Assessment Meeting (MIAM) unless they are exempt from doing so e.g. where domestic violence is involved or the application is urgent. **Section 10(1) Children and families Act 2014.**

An application for a grandparent is no exception. If the parties do not attend for mediation, they face the possibility of an adjournment of the first hearing in order to attend mediation.

If mediation is unsuccessful, the grandparent will file an application to the court for permission.

Forms and Filing

Usually, this is by using a **Form C2** together with a **Form C100**. It is important that written reasons for an order are set out in detail. The applicant must attach an additional sheet to the application form if there is insufficient space on the form. In practice, this means the applicant will file both an application for permission **and** the substantive application at the same time.

If there are allegations of violence or safety, Form C1A should be submitted and if an address is to be withheld, then Form C8 should also be submitted.

Draft Order

A copy of the draft order should be enclosed for permission when filing the court papers. The **CAP forms under the Standard Family Orders [2018] Family Law 371** set out the wording for court orders and are used by most courts and easy to use.

Court Fees

A court fee is payable at the time of filing application forms.

A client may be exempt from paying the court fee due to their limited financial circumstances. If so, **Form Ex 160** should be filed on filing the papers with the court.

The court fee is a "one off" payment. If permission is granted, no further fee is payable on the filing of the **Form C100.**

Service of papers & Court hearing

The court will fix a date for the **permission application** to be dealt with.

All parties with parental responsibility will be served with the application and invited to attend that initial hearing for permission.

If permission is granted, the Section 8 application will proceed and a further date given to hear that matter.

It should be noted that no Safeguarding Checks will be undertaken by Cafcass in relation to the **permission** application. Safeguarding Checks will only take place once permission to apply has been granted by the court.

Once permission is granted, the court will fix a hearing date for the Section 8 substantive application and activate the Safeguarding checks in the meantime.

Wording of the Order for Permission

The is found in the CAP forms as found in the Standard Family Orders [2018] Family Law 371 as follows:

The (name of grandparent) has permission to apply for (select which of the following applies)

- a Child Arrangements Order;
- a Prohibited Steps Order;
- a Specific Issue Order;
- a Special Guardianship Order.

In or Out of Proceedings

An application for Permission to file will be sought either:

- In **Existing proceedings** – possibly where parents are in dispute over their child or perhaps more commonly, in care proceedings

- or as a **Freestanding Application** often used in private proceedings

If there are already ongoing proceedings, an application by a grandparent can be filed within those proceedings, using **Form C2.**

If there are no existing proceedings, the application will be a **Freestanding application** and both Forms **C2** and **C100** will need be filed.

Parental Responsibility

Grandparent client cannot gain Parental Responsibility **without** having a Court order.

There is no such thing as a Parental Responsibility Order or Agreement for a grandparent.

The usual orders giving a grandparent Parental Responsibility would be a **Child Arrangements Order or a Special Guardianship Order.**

Parental Responsibility in favour of the grandparent will last as long as the court order is in existence. If the court order comes to an end, so does Parental Responsibility.

CHAPTER NINE

APPLICATIONS FOR LEAVE BY THE CHILD CONCERNED

A grandchild may express a wish to live with his/her grandparent. Usually, a child is not entitled to apply for a Section 8 order or for an order varying or discharging such an order, concerning himself. He will need the permission of the court to apply. He may be granted permission if the court is satisfied that he has sufficient understanding to make the application and able to participate as a party in the proceedings.

The general rule is that, if he is the subject of the proceedings, a child cannot make an application or be joined as a party, unless he has a Children's Guardian. Where he is not the subject of the proceedings, a Litigation Friend should conduct the proceedings on his behalf.

It is a matter of fact as to whether the child is of sufficient age and understanding.

Re S (A Minor) (Independent Representation) 1993 3 All ER 36 at 43-44

If a child, of sufficient understanding, makes an application for permission to file a Section 8 order, and the court is satisfied that his father/mother can adequately represent his views, the court is likely to refuse the child's application.

Re H (Residence Order: Childs application for Leave) (2000) 1FLR 780 FD

A clear distinction must be drawn between a case where the child applicant is the subject of the proceedings, and where he is not. For example, if the applicant is a teenager having given birth to a child, then **Section 10(9)** will apply.

Procedure where a child seeks permission

In the case of a child seeking permission to file a section 8 order, the Family Procedure Rules 2010 **rule16.6** permits applications to be brought without a Litigation Friend or Children's Guardian either with permissions of the court or where a solicitor, having considered the child is able to have sufficient understanding to give instructions, has accepted those instructions. In both situations the test of whether the child has sufficient understanding is the same as under **section 10(8).** The responsibility for assessing the child's competence rests with the solicitor although the court retains a discretion to determine the child's capacity.

Re T (A minor)(child representation (1994) 4 All E R 518

Applications for permission can be made without notice but where a child is the applicant, it is desirable that everyone with parental responsibility is given notice **Per Booth J in Re SC (A Minor) (Leave to seek Residence Order) 1994 1 FLR 96.**

CHAPTER TEN

FUNDING AN APPLICATION TO THE COURT

There are four possible ways an application may be funded:

1. Legal Aid

Legal aid funding is rarely available for most cases involving a grandparent. If a grandparent has been subjected to domestic violence from a parent, legal aid may be available but subject to a means test. These cases are likely to be rare.

2. Personal Funding

A client will almost certainly need to consider raising your legal fees personally. This can be a barrier or many applicants. The client may qualify for exemption of payment the court fee on the basis their limited means by filing Form EX160.

3. Local Authority Funding

If the Local Authority are involved in some way with the grandchild in question, it may be that they will agree to provide some funding for the grandparent to apply to the court. It can be seen as a cheaper option to financially support a grandparent in private proceedings rather than commence public law proceedings themselves. Some Local Authorities are more generous than others.

Some Local Authorities will be willing to pay the full costs, while others will limit payment to a few hours of legal advice only. This needs checking at an early stage.

4. The Grandparent acting as a Litigant in Person

If all other means of funding fail, the grandparent has the option of dealing with the application personally, as a Litigant in Person. The grandparent's financial circumstances may exempt him/her from paying the court fee by using Form EX160 and the grandparent will complete the court forms and attend any court hearings without legal representation. Courts are becoming accustomed to parties in proceedings acting on their own behalf. The court will assist a Litigant in Person in presenting their case. The court staff are not able to advise a party on how to conduct their case nor to advise on any point of law or procedure.

A word of caution

It goes without saying that disputes over grandchildren should be settled outside the court arena, if at all possible.

Discussions within the family and, if necessary, Mediation are the best way of resolving such disputes.

It is only as a very last resort that disputed issues involving a grandparent should be put before the Court. Any application to the court will carry with it not only the risk of legal costs but emotional costs too.

CHAPTER ELEVEN

PUBLIC LAW PROCEEDINGS

Public Proceedings are where the Local Authority Social Services Department are involved with a grandchild.

If a child is at risk of "**significant harm**" under either **Sections 31 or 38 of the Children Act 1989** the Local Authority are obliged to take steps to protect that child from such risk. **Sections 17 & 47 Children Act 1989** and **Section 11 Children Act 2004.**

This will sometimes mean that the child is removed from the care of the parents and placed with an alternative carer.

This can be to place a child with a paid foster carer often by way of a Care Order under **Sections 31 and 38 of the Children Act 1989** or sometimes by agreement with the parent under **Section 20 the same Act.**

As an alternative to a foster placement, the Local Authority are obliged to consider placing a child with a "**Kinship Carer**" as set out in **Section 22 Children Act 1989.**

A "**Kinship Carer**" can be a grandparent and they are often the first "port of call" for the placement of their grandchild.

This placement can take place under a Child Arrangements Order (possibly for a fixed period) during the Care proceedings. They may also be assessed as Foster parents.

If Care proceedings are continuing, it may be to a grandparent's advantage to care for the grandchild under a Child Arrangements Order.

The Child Arrangements Order will give the grandparent parental responsibility and will also give them access to legal aid, on a non-means and non-merits basis. As a result, legal representation is free of charge.

The grandparent will become a party within the Care proceedings and thus have access to all the papers in the case, able to attend court with his/her own solicitor, and be actively involved in the care proceedings relating to the grandchild.

The Local Authority will, of course, need to undertake a Viability assessment of the grandparent to satisfy themselves and the court that the grandparent is a suitable carer.

Some Local Authorities may not be willing to consent to the grandparent having party status in the proceedings or being granted a Child Arrangement Order until a viability assessment has been completed.

CHAPTER TWELVE

GRANDPARENTS' CONTACT WITH THEIR GRANDCHILDREN IN THE CARE OF A LOCAL AUTHORITY

If a child is living with a foster carer under a Care order, the grandparent does not have an automatic right to see the grandchild. The exception to this would be if the grandparent has parental responsibility for the child. If the Local Authority are not willing to allow the grandchild contact with the grandparent, the grandparent can apply to the court, within the Care proceedings, for an order under **Section 34(1) of the Children Act. Permission to apply** for an order is still necessary. If, however, the grandparent has parental responsibility in respect of their grandchild prior to being placed in care, the Local Authority must allow contact to continue in some form unless an order is made stating otherwise.

In the event that the grandparent has no automatic right to contact, a possible compromise could be for the grandparent to see the grandchild at the same time as a parent.

Under **Section 34(1) Children Act 1989**, Children's Services must allow the child **reasonable contact** with:

- his parents;

- any guardian;
- any person who held a Residence Order or Child Arrangements Order for residence immediately before the Care Order was made; and
- any person who had care of the child under wardship immediately before the Care Order was made.

Children's Services has a general duty to promote contact with wider family members such as grandparents and siblings under **Schedule 2(15) Children Act 1989** which states:

Promotion and maintenance of contact between child and family

(1) Where a child is being looked after by a local authority, the authority shall, unless it is not reasonably practicable or consistent with his welfare, endeavour to promote contact between the child and—

(a) his parents;

(b) any person who is not a parent of his but who has parental responsibility for him; and

(c) any relative, friend or other person connected with him.

(2) Where a child is being looked after by a local authority—

(a) the authority shall take such steps as are reasonably practicable to secure that—

(i) his parents; and

(ii) any person who is not a parent of his but who has parental responsibility for him,

are kept informed of where he is being accommodated; and

(b) every such person shall secure that the authority are kept informed of his or her address.

This is the default position in the absence of any court orders.

What if a child is not looked after in the care system during proceedings?

Some children may be subject to care proceedings, but not looked after in the care system. Examples include a grandparent or aunt caring for the child under a child arrangements order.

In this situation, the legal duties which are in place in relation to contact for looked after children would not apply. Instead, arrangements about contact may be agreed between the parent and the person who is caring for the child.

But those arrangements should still be:

- Agreed with the children's services
- Included in the child's care plan
- Approved by the court dealing with the proceedings.

Note if a relative in caring for a child under a care order or under a voluntary arrangement (under **section 20 of the Children Act 1989**) they will be a kinship foster carer and the child will be a looked after child.

Will the wider family and friends network still be able to have contact with a looked after child during care proceedings?

Unless it is not in the child's best interests, children's services must promote contact between a child who is looked after under a court order and:

- Their parents
- Anyone else who has parental responsibility for them, and
- Any relative, friend or other person connected with them

when a child is looked after under a court order.

Government statutory guidance **The Children Act 1989 guidance and regulations: Volume 2: care planning, placement and case review** reminds children's services of the importance of maintaining relationships between children and their wider family and friends network.

This says:

- 'In discussions with the child during the assessment and as part of wider considerations, it will be important to identify all those people in the child's network with whom it is important to maintain contact. They may not always be blood relatives of the child' (**paragraph 2.81**)
- 'Grandparents and other relatives can provide a sense of family history and continuity where the child cannot live with his/her

birth parents yet contact may easily be lost if the child becomes looked after' (**paragraph 2.84**).

The precise duties will depend on whether the child is looked after under a voluntary arrangement or under a court order.

An application for contact to the court is made using a **C1 form**, or if court proceedings have already started, you can use a **C2 form.** You will also need the **C15 supplement form.**

The courts must take into account the following principles when deciding to grant contact or change the terms of a current contact arrangement:

- If the contact is in the child's best interests
- Reasonable contact between the parents and child should continue
- The application is part of an effort to set aside a care order
- Parents (or others making the application) can show a change of circumstances which the local authority should have acknowledged when putting together the child's care plan

The only exceptions to this legal duty are: if there has been an incident of some kind which the local authority thinks is serious enough to stop contact, or if the quality of contact between you and your child has got worse over a long period of time.

The local authority can then pause contact for up to 7 days. However it still cannot stop contact for more than 7 days, or indefinitely, without a court order.

CHAPTER THIRTEEN

SPECIAL GUARDIANSHIP ORDERS

These are an invention of **Section 115 of the Adoption and Children Act 2002** and became **Section 14A of the Children Act 1989.**

Such orders have been available to the courts since the 30th December 2005 and have increased in use over the years. Even though they are private law orders they are more frequently made in public law proceedings.

Sometimes circumstances arise in which children are not able to live with their parents and have to be cared for by someone else. It may be a relative (eg grandparent) or a friend or it could be a foster carer who works for the Local Authority. These arrangements may be for a short or long period and may be made by the parents and the new carer directly or a social worker may be involved. If there is a plan for a child to live with someone other than the parents in the long term, the arrangements may be secured by a court order.

Two most common orders are:

- **a Child Arrangement Order** which sets out who the child will live with and also details of who the child should spend time with previously known as contact;

- **a Special Guardianship Order** available to non-parents.

A Special Guardianship Order is an order appointing one or more individuals to be a child's 'special guardian'. It is a private law order made under the Children Act 1989 and is intended for those children who cannot live with their birth parents and who would benefit from a legally secure placement.

It is a more secure order than a Child Arrangement Order but less than an Adoption Order because it does not end the legal relationship between the child and his/her birth parents.

Special Features of a Special Guardianship Order

1. It is a "halfway house" between a Child Arrangements Order and an Adoption Order.

2. The order is available to anyone (including grandparents) other than a parent of the child in question.

3. It is often used by the courts to secure a placement with a grandparent following care proceedings.

4. The carer (in our case, the grandparent) becomes a **Special Guardian.**

5. The child concerned remains in the community and often within the family but not with the parent.

6. It avoids an adoption which would bring any formal relationships with the family to an end.

7. The order remains in place until the child is 18 years of age unless discharged earlier. The usual end day for a Residence Order or Child Arrangements Order is 16 years

8. For parents, it means that they can usually keep in contact with their child.

9. The making of a Special Guardianship Order discharges a Care Order **Schedule 3 ACA 2002.**

10. A Special Guardianship Order gives the Special Guardian parental responsibility during the existence of the order.

11. If the Special Guardianship Order comes to an end for some reason, so does parental responsibility for the Special Guardian.

12. One particular feature is that the order gives the Special Guardian greater control over the care and upbringing of the child, at the expense of the parents. Whilst parents retain parental responsibility, this is reduced to the extent that they will only need to be consulted by the Special Guardian on issues of a change of name and removal from the court's jurisdiction for a period of more than three months. Contact between the grandchild and the parents often takes place but is at the behest of the Special Guardian.

13. The Special Guardian can appoint a testamentary Guardian to look after the child if the Special Guardian dies before the child reaches 18 years of age. The person appointed will share parental responsibility with the birth parent;

14. The Special Guardian must notify the parents if the child dies;

15. The Special Guardian Order also carries with it the right to receive help from the Local Authority in the form of counselling and other support.

16. The Special Guardian can also seek financial help from the Local Authority. A means test is involved to assess the grandparents' needs under the **Special Guardianship Regulations 2005.**

The Wording of the Order

This is found in the CAP form under the Standard Family Orders [2018] Family Law 371:

(Names of grandparents) are appointed as Special Guardians in respect of (Names of children).

How does the Grandparent obtain a Special Guardianship Order?

1. Written notice should given to the Local Authority by the proposed carer requesting that she/he is assessed for the purposes of a Special Guardianship Order. Such notice is given to the Local Authority in whose area the child resides.

2. This notice gives the Local Authority **three-months notice** of the client's intention to apply for a Special Guardianship Order.

3. There is **no set form** of notice but will need to contain details of the client's name, address, name and date of birth, the address of the child, the client's relationship to the child and a request that the Local Authority undertake an assessment to enable the client to apply for a Special Guardianship Order.

4. This Notice will trigger a detailed assessment of the client by the Local Authority.

5. The client will need to be prepared for a full enquiry which will look at the family history, health and ability to care for the grandchild.

6. A report will be presented to the client who may wish to make an application to the court for a Special Guardianship Order at that stage. The application will be served on all those who have parental responsibility for the child in question and a hearing date is fixed.

7. The court can make a Special Guardianship Order of its own motion provided it has a report to consider.

8. The Special Guardianship Order will continue unto the child reaches 18 years of age unless varied before that date.

Special Guardianship in Private Proceedings

A grandparent can apply for a Special Guardianship Order **as a private application** i.e. when there are no other proceedings such as Care or Supervision proceedings, without seeking the courts permission if:

1. The grandparent already has a Residence Order or a Child Arrangements Order (living with arrangement);

2. The child has lived with the grandparent for **three out of the five years prior to the application;**

3. If the child is already in the care of the Local Authority and the Local Authority **supports the application;**

4. The grandparent has the **consent of all those with parental responsibility;**

5. The grandparent is a **foster carer** and the child has **lived them for one year or more;**

6. In any event, with the court's permission;

Contrast between Child Arrangements Order and a Special Guardianship Order

A Child Arrangements Order is potentially a long-term order settling the arrangements to be made as to the person with whom a child is to live and gives the holder Parental Responsibility. The exercise of that responsibility is a matter for agreement with others who hold it. Commonly, one parent has a Child Arrangements Order providing for the child to live with her and the other has contact. If a Child Arrangement Order is made in favour of grandparents providing for a grandchild to live with them, contact in favour of the parents is often set out in the order.

A Special Guardianship Order cements the relationship between the Special Guardian and the child to a greater degree than a Child Arrangements Order. Parental responsibility under a Special Guardianship Order is exercised exclusively by the Special Guardian. The only areas which require the Special Guardian to consult with others with Parental Responsibility involve consent to adoption, change of name, or removal from the jurisdiction for more than three months. The court making a Special Guardianship Order must first consider whether it is in the interests of the child to make a Child Arrangements Order rather than a SGO.

Variation of a Special Guardianship Order

If circumstances change significantly, a court can vary or discharge a Special Guardianship Order under **Section 14 D Children Act 1989.**

Parents require the court's permission before making this application. The court will need to be satisfied that there has been a significant change in circumstances since the order was made. Applying for permission is a two-stage process. If the applicant is granted permission, the court will then go on consider the welfare of the child and whether it is in the interest of the child to vary or discharge the Special Guardianship Order.

An application by a Special Guardian, or any person who is named on a Child Arrangements Order as the person with whom the child is to live or a Local Authority in whose name a Care Order was in force before the Special Guardianship Order was made do not need prior permission to apply for a variation or discharge.

Discharge or Variation of a Special Guardianship Order – recent developments

Unlike an adoption order, the court may vary or discharge a Special Guardianship Order on the application of :

- A Special Guardian (or one of them, if more than one);
- A parent / guardian of child;
- Any person with a residence order in force;
- Any other person who had parental responsibility for the child immediately before the Special Guardianship Order was made;

- The child;

- A Local Authority which has a Care Order.

However, an application to *discharge the order* cannot be made by certain people unless the court has given them *permission* to do so. These people include:

- The child concerned (provided they have sufficient understanding of the proposed application);

- A parent/guardian;

- A step-parent who has parental responsibility under Section 4A of the Children Act 1989;

- Any other person who had parental responsibility for the child immediately *before* the Special Guardianship Order was made.

So parents who wish to apply to discharge an SGO in order to recover the care of the child must obtain the court's permission.

The *first stage* is that a parent who wishes to obtain permission to apply to discharge the SGO must show a *significant change in circumstances.* If a parent cannot show a *significant change in circumstances* their application will fail. If a parent shows there is a *significant change in circumstances* the court has to go on to *stage two*. The court will only *give permission* for an application to discharge the order if it is satisfied that there has been a *significant change of circumstances* since the Special Guardianship Order was made. The only exception to this is when it is the child who is seeking leave to apply for a discharge.

At *stage two* the court will decide whether leave should be granted, based on a realistic evaluation of the applicant's prospects of success in the context of the effect on the child's welfare of the application being heard or not heard. The prospects of success must be real. The child's welfare is an important factor but it is not the paramount consideration. The degree of any change in circumstances is likely to be intertwined with the prospects of success, and the greater the prospects of success, the more likely it is that leave will be granted.

A Court of Appeal case which concerned *the test* for granting leave to apply to discharge a special guardianship order and the construction of Section14D(5) of the Children Act 1989:

The proceedings in ***Re M (Special Guardianship Order: Leave to Apply to Discharge)*** [2021] EWCA Civ 442 concerned C, a boy aged 9. The father was never present, and the mother had serious mental health problems which resulted in C moving to live with his maternal grandmother and her partner (the grandparents) when he was aged 4½. The local authority concluded that the mother could meet C's needs when she was well, but not when she was ill. A special guardianship order was subsequently made in favour of the grandparents without opposition. Directions were given detailing contact arrangements between C and the mother.

In February 2020, the mother applied for leave to make an application to discharge the SGO. She made a further application for a Child Arrangements Order in July 2020 for C to spend time with her while the proceedings continued. The mother submitted that her mental health had greatly improved. However, the grandparents argued that it would not be in C's interests to have a change of care. The local authority expressed concerns over the special guardianship order being revoked in that it could impact upon C's stability.

The Judge concluded that even though there had been changes in the mother's circumstances, it was not in C's welfare interests to reopen proceedings. Further, due to multiple concerns about the mother's ability to care for C and the risk of C's life becoming unstable, the Judge considered that it would be very difficult for the mother's application to succeed. Therefore, the application for leave to apply to discharge the SGO was dismissed, with the Judge citing her paramount consideration in this decision being C's welfare. In relation to the contact application, the Judge also concluded that it was not in C's welfare interests to have a contact order as it could cause more harm and tension between the adults and for C to become confused. Therefore, this application was dismissed.

The Court outlined that the legal status of special guardianship was created to offer 'greater security for children than long-term fostering but without the absolute legal severance from the birth family that stems from adoption.'

Section 14D of the Children Act 1989 concerns the manner in which SGOs can be varied or discharged. A parent seeking to discharge an SGO requires leave of the court which can only be given if the court is satisfied that there has been a significant change in circumstances. In regards to what a 'significant change of circumstances 'meant, the Court cited the case of **Re G (Special *Guardianship Order) [2010] EWCA Civ 300***, in which it was held that the two-stage test developed in the case of ***M v Warwickshire County Council [2007] EWCA Civ 1084*** applied, despite that test concerning applications for leave to revoke a placement order.

The first limb is that there must have been a significant change in circumstances. The Court considered that significant simply means 'considerable, noteworthy or important'. The second limb is that there must be a real prospect of success. It was concluded that the degree of the change of circumstances is interlinked with this limb and the greater the prospects of success, the 'more cogent the welfare arguments must be if leave is refused. 'However, the welfare of the child is not the paramount consideration of the second limb, as it is considered later, in deciding whether to allow the application.

In relation to the mother's application for parental contact, the Court outlined that when an SGO is in effect, a parent does not need leave to apply for such an order. The case of ***Re S (Adoption Order or Special Guardianship Order) [2007] EWCA Civ 54*** was cited, where it was submitted by the foster mother seeking an adoption order, that one of her reasons for preferring adoption was because it gave protection from applications being made by the child's mother. The present Court concluded at [38] that 'there is nothing objectionable in principle about a contact application issued in respect of a child subject to an SGO.'

It was submitted by the mother, within 9 grounds of appeal, that the bar for special guardianship orders to be revoked was set too high as it made it a near impossible. In particular, she argued that the Judge erred in treating C's welfare as paramount, the Judge had no basis for saying that if permission was given there would be another set of care proceedings and a risk of C being put in foster care. She further argued that the Judge was wrong to dismiss the application for contact without taking into account that contact had not taken place in accordance with the working agreement.

On behalf of the grandparents, it was submitted that the Judge was entitled to refuse leave and her decision was not one which the court should interfere with. Further, it was argued that the mother's progress had not been substantial enough.

The Court of Appeal said the Judge's test for change in circumstances was too high as she held that a guarantee was required that all the issues leading to the SGO had been resolved; concluded that the appeal should succeed for the following reasons:

The Judge's conclusion flowed directly from the test she had set;

1. The Judge was not in a position to reach the conclusion she did about the mother's mental health, because a deeper assessment was required;

2. The judge did not make any real assessment of the mother's prospects of success;

3. The comments regarding the risk of foster care were inappropriate;

4. The Judge favoured the grandparents 'view of how the working agreement of contact was working without having enough evidence to make this conclusion;

5. The Judge did not look at welfare correctly, as the SGO is not currently providing C with the necessary sense of security, stability and belonging required; and

6. There was no good reason for the summary dismissal of the mother's application.

The appeal was accordingly allowed, and the previous orders set aside. The mother was granted leave to apply to discharge the SGO and restore her application for contact.

Contact

Unlike applications to discharge the SGO, contact applications *do not need permission*. The Court of Appeal said a parent has an unfettered right to apply for contact with a child subject to an SGO and that this is an important detraction from the overriding parental responsibility possessed by special guardians. However, the court has the power to restrain unmeritorious applications by making orders under **s. 91(14)**. But in the normal run of events, there is nothing objectionable in principle about a contact application issued in respect of a child subject to an SGO [pa 38]

Summarising the reasons for allowing the appeal, the Court of Appeal said the judge had taken great care in considering the case and setting out her reasons, but ultimately had set too high a test for permission and had wrongly jumped to conclusions at too early a stage. She had also wrongly treated the child's welfare as 'paramount' (it was important but not 'paramount').

The Court of Appeal's observation that the judge failed to look at welfare in the round – and had she done so she might have seen that the case 'cried out' for investigation and remedy, whether that is achieved by a change of attitude on the part of the family members, or by the fortification of the SGO, or by its discharge. The outcome of the Judge's decision is that none of these will happen and the family is left to carry on as it is. In a situation in which inaction is not an option, the Judge did not appreciate that the mother's applications offered an opportunity to resolve the current difficulties and she did not factor this important consideration into her thinking at the second stage. She instead focused exclusively on her concern about proceedings making a bad situation worse in the short term, without taking account of how the situation might be improved in the medium to long term by investigation and resolution.

[pa 52]

Re F & G (Discharge of Special Guardianship Order) [2021] EWCA Civ 622

The Court of Appeal confirmed that a Special Guardianship Order can co-exist with a Care Order and remitted for re-hearing the question of whether or not the SGO in this case should be discharged.

Background

The mother (M) of twin girls born in 2010 formed a relationship with K during the pregnancy and the girls grew up believing him to be their father; they had no contact with their biological father. M and K later married, divorcing in 2017. After M formed a relationship with a violent man, the LA issued care proceedings, placing the children with K under ICOs in April 2019.

K was assessed as having extremely low cognitive ability and although he coped well with the children he needed considerable support. An SGO assessment was positive; despite his learning disability he had evidenced his ability to meet the children's emotional needs. At the final hearing of the care proceedings in April 2020 all parties agreed to the making of an SGO in favour of K and a full care order to the LA. No judgment was delivered giving the reasons for this outcome.

The placement with K broke down a few weeks later and the LA gave notice of their intention to remove the children to foster care. K applied to discharge the care orders and unsuccessfully applied for an injunction preventing the girls' removal. Following the children's placement with foster carers the LA initially sought the discharge of the SGO on the basis that K no longer needed PR. By the final hearing however the LA and guardian thought the SGO should remain in place despite there being no plan for the children to return to K. M had, without the necessary permission, filed an application to discharge the SGO. Rather than considering whether the test for permission was met the judge heard argument about whether the SGO should remain in place on the basis of the court's power pursuant to s14D(2) CA 1989. He refused to discharge the SGO but attached a condition limiting K's power to seek information from third parties while the care order was in force.

The appeal

The first ground of appeal was that SGOs and care orders cannot exist in law. This was rejected because the amendments to the Children Act 1989 made when SGOs were introduced clearly do allow for this situation:

- **S91** makes it crystal clear that an SGO is not automatically discharged by the making of a final care order.
- **S33(3)(b)(i)**, as amended, allows a LA to determine the extent to which a "parent, guardian or special guardian" may exercise PR when a care order is in force. This demonstrates Parliament's intention that an SGO could continue after the making of a care order.
- The provisions of s14D which entitle a LA designated in a care order to apply for the discharge of an SGO would be pointless if a care order operated to discharge a pre-existing SGO. The SGO must continue unless and until discharged.

- SGOs are intended to provide long-term support for the child and it would be contrary to the purpose of special guardianship if SGOs came to an end automatically on the making of a care order; whether or not they should remain in force depends on the circumstances and must be decided in accordance with the child's welfare.

The second ground, that the judge was wrong to refuse to discharge the SGO, raised more complex issues. There were welfare arguments in both directions. The judge had been particularly concerned that the children should maintain links with K, who had been treated as their father and was an important person in their lives. He worried that over time the LA might cease to communicate with him and his relationship with the children could be undermined. His attention was not drawn to an option which emerged during the appeal hearing, namely to make an order for contact under s34(2) and to invite the LA to amend its care plan to contain an express provision that K fell within the category of persons identified in s22(4), namely a person whose wishes and feelings it considered relevant when making decisions about all matters concerning the children's future. A well drafted care plan could have provided substantial protection for the children's relationship with K and his involvement in decision-making.

The CA was uneasy about allowing a decision to stand that had been arrived at "after an unsatisfactory process without full consideration of the options". Accordingly the decision was set aside and the matter remitted to the trial judge for rehearing.

Re: F & G Take Away Points:

- A Care Order can be made in respect of a child whom is already subject to a Special Guardianship Order

- The court must consider whether the outcome can be achieved by a more orthodox means
- This is the first authority that definitively confirms that it is possible for Care Orders and Special Guardianships Orders to exist as a package of final orders.

What can a parent do if there is a dispute with the Special Guardian about a decision concerning the child?

If a parent does not agree with any decision a Special Guardian has made regarding their child, the parent should to try and speak to the Special Guardian and explain their point of view and their reasons. If this is difficult, mediation is a possibility with the Special Guardian to see if an agreement can be reached.

If mediation is unsuccessful then the last option would be to apply either for a Specific Issue Order, asking the court to determine the issue or a Prohibited steps Order, asking the court to issue an order preventing the Special Guardian from doing something, e.g. taking the child abroad.

Who can apply for Special Guardianship Orders?

The applicant must be over 18 years of age and cannot be the parent of the child in question. The applicant can make an application on his/her own or jointly with another person. The following people may apply to be special guardians:

- Any guardian of the child.
- Those who have a Child Arrangements Order or a Residence Order for the child.

- Anyone with whom the child has lived for at least three years out of the last five years.

- Anyone with the consent of the local authority if the child is in care.

- A local authority foster parent with whom the child has lived for at least one year preceding the application.

- A relative of the child and the child has resided with them for at least one year immediately pre-dating an application for a Special Guardianship Order

- Anyone who has the consent of those with the **parental responsibility**.

- Anyone who has permission of the Court to make the application.

What is the role of the local authority?

The **Special Guardianship Regulations 2005** state that the local authority report should include certain key information about the child such as:

- Whether the child has brothers and sisters and details of both parents.

- The relationship a child has with other family members and the arrangements for the child to see or keep in touch with different family members.

- Details of the child's relationship with his/her parents.

- The parent/s' and the child's wishes and feelings.
- The prospective Guardian's family composition and circumstances
- Parenting capacity of the Guardian.
- Medical information on the child, prospective special guardian and the birth parent(s).
- An assessment of how a Special Guardianship Order would meet a child's long-term interests as compared with other types of order.
- A recommendation regarding contact and Special Guardianship.
- Implications of the making of the Special Guardianship Order for all those involved.

Each local authority must make arrangements for the provision of special guardianship support services which may include:

- Financial assistance (means tested).
- Assistance with the arrangements for contact between a child, his/her parents and any relatives that the local authority consider to be beneficial.
- This assistance can include cash to help with the cost of travel, entertainment, and mediation to help resolve difficulties on contact.
- Respite care.

- Counselling, advice, information and other support services.
- Services to enable children, parents and special guardians to discuss matters, this might include setting up a support group.
- Therapeutic services for the child.

What happens after an assessment?

This assessment determines whether a person has a need for special support services and whether the Local Authority can offer this service. The person should be given notice and information of the support offered and if appropriate the financial support too.

What about financial support?

It may be possible to make an application to the Local Authority for a **Special Guardianship Allowance**. Local Authorities will then have to work out how much fostering allowance would have been paid had the child been fostered rather than cared for under a Special Guardianship Order.

What kind of support is available to a Special Guardian?

Under the **Adoption and Children Act 2002**, financial support and other services may be available for the Special Guardian, the child and the parent(s). However, if a child is not (or was not) looked after by a Local Authority, then there is no automatic entitlement to an assessment for Special Guardianship Support services. It is possible to request an assessment for support in this situation.

Examples of possible services include:

- mediation to assist with new or existing contact arrangements;
- counselling and advice and information;
- access to support groups;
- therapy services;
- training for the special guardian to meet the needs of the child;
- respite care; and
- financial assistance. Biological parents remain financially responsible in engineering for their child even when a Special Guardianship Order has been issued, so in most cases they will be under an obligation to pay maintenance for the child's upbringing.

Can a client ask for an assessment to be carried out for support services?

The Local Authority must provide an assessment for support services to a parent, special guardian or child in relation to a child **who is looked after** by the Local Authority. If the child was in the care of a different Local Authority immediately before the Special Guardianship Order was granted, the original Local Authority should be contacted as they are responsible for assessing the support needs for the three years following the Special Guardianship Order being made.

If the child in question is not a looked after child, the following people can request an assessment from their Local Authority for support services:

- the child;
- the Special Guardian;
- a parent;
- a child of the Special Guardian ;
- any person that the Local Authority considers has a significant and ongoing relationship with the child.

However it will be the decision of the Local Authority whether they decide to carry out an assessment. Once a request has been made, the Local Authority must inform the applicant of their decision in writing and include reasons. There is then 28 days to respond to the decision.

What will the assessment for support services involve?

The assessment undertaken by the Local Authority will consider:

- the developmental needs of the child;
- the parenting capacity of the Special Guardian;
- the family and environmental factors which have shaped the life of the child;
- what the life of the child might be like with the Special Guardian;
- any previous assessment undertaken; and the needs of the Special Guardian and their family. It is possible to apply to the Local Authority for a Special Guardianship Allowance.

What will happen after an assessment for support services has taken place?

The assessment will determine whether a person has a need for special support services. Where the Local Authority decides to offer support services, they should give the person notice of the services they intend to offer including, if applicable, the amount of financial support. The person should have the opportunity at this point to make representations regarding the proposed support. It is advisable to seek independent legal advice before any provision is agreed.

Is assistance available in cash?

Regulation 3(2) states that a local authority can provide assistance in cash to a Special Guardian. For example:

- money to pay for a babysitter to provide respite for an evening; or
- money for petrol to facilitate a contact visit.

This kind of assistance should not be means tested as it is being provided as part of a service rather than financial support.

What financial support is available?

It is possible to apply to the Local Authority for a Special Guardianship Allowance. The allowance is means-tested but guidance is given in the **Special Guardianship Regulations 2005**. These Regulations direct Local Authorities to have regard to how much fostering allowance would have been paid had the child been fostered rather than cared for under a Special Guardianship Order. Recent case engineering confirms that the rate for Special Guardianship

Allowances should be calculated in line with fostering allowances. Deductions may be made to take into account Child Benefit and Tax Credit.

When can financial support be provided to the Special Guardian?

Regulation 6 sets out when financial support can be provided by the Local Authority:

- when it is necessary to enable a Special Guardian to look after a child;
- when a child needs special care due to disability, emotional or behaviour difficulties or previous neglect or abuse;
- to help towards the legal costs for applying for a Special Guardianship Order, a Child Arrangements Order, a Prohibited Steps Order, a Specific Issue Order, or for applying for a financial provision for the child; and
- when it is necessary to contribute towards the cost of accommodating and maintaining a child.

What does a financial assessment involve?

The Local Authority will usually consider the Special Guardian's means; **Regulation 13** of the guidance requires that the Local Authority consider:

- the financial resources of the Special Guardian;
- the amount required in respect of reasonable outgoings and commitments; and

- the financial needs that relate to the child.

If a Local Authority supports a person's application for Special Guardianship for a looked after child, they must not take into account the person's means when considering providing financial support for legal costs.

What support can *a child* receive under Special Guardianship Order?

Children who were looked after by the Local Authority immediately before the making of a Special Guardianship Order may qualify for advice and assistance under **section 24 Children Act 1989.** The child must:

- have reached the age of 16, but not the age of 21;
- have a Special Guardianship Order in force if less than 18 years old;
- have had a Special Guardianship Order in force when they reached the age of 18;
- have been looked after by a local authority immediately before the making of the Special Guardianship Order.

If a child meets these criteria, then the Local Authority which last looked after the child is under a duty to provide advice and assistance.

Fair Access Limit

The **Adoption Support Fund** pays for a range of therapeutic support for adopted children and their adoptive family. Since April 2017, this has been extended to include children cared for by special guardians who were 'looked after' immediately before the Special Guardianship Order was granted.

To request financial support under the fair access limit, a request for an assessment will have to be made to the Local Authority. Where the assessment determines that therapeutic services would be required by the child, the Local Authority will apply to the Adoption Support Fund on the client's behalf. A fair access limit of £5,000 has recently been introduced.

CHAPTER FOURTEEN

SPECIAL GUARDIANSHIP ORDER CHANGES

1. Following the implementation of the **Adoption and Children Act 2002 (amending the Children Act 1989 (section 14 A-G))** the courts have had the ability to make Special Guardianship Orders since December 2005. **Section 14A (3)(a) Children Act 1989** sets out the power of the court to make a Special Guardianship Order when an application is made by a person eligible to do so. **Section 14A (3)(b)** contains the power where that individual has obtained the leave of the court to apply.

2. The Court may also make a Special Guardianship Order with respect to a child **in any family proceedings** in which a question arises with respect to the welfare of the child.

3. A review of Special Guardianship Orders was undertaken in 2015 by the government which focused on concerns relating rushed or poor quality assessments, potentially risky placements being made and inadequate support for Special Guardians. The review caused amendments to be made to the Special Guardianship Regulations 2005, through the Special Guardianship (Amendment) Regulations 2016. Those amendments were aimed at strengthening the Special Guardianship Orders assessment process and in particular to ensure that any harm the child had experienced was identified

and that the capacity of the prospective Special Guardians to address consequences arising from those issues in the parenting of the child were considered.

4. The case of **P-S (Children) [2018] EWCA Civ 1407** highlighted the ongoing need for further clarification as Special Guardianship Orders have evolved. The Court of Appeal gave general guidance on the approach to be taken in consideration of Special Guardians and the making of Special Guardianship Orders within care proceedings. The President of the Family Division, who gave a separate judgment, argued that there was a real need for alternative guidance to sit alongside the statutory materials and invited the Family Judge Council to undertake such a test.

5. In June 2020 a **Public Law Working Group** made recommendations to achieve best practice in relation to Special Guardianship Orders. The report highlighted that a number of controversies had emerged in recent years about the use of Special Guardianship Orders:

   > "These are mainly whether the courts are giving Local Authorities and potential Special Guardians sufficient time for full assessments to be undertaken and for everyone to fully understand the implications and effects if the order is to be made, which will last until the child turns. Associated with the above issues the guidance highlighted that Special Guardians receive minimal advice and support from Local Authorities compared with foster carers, although there is little to distinguish between the extent of children's welfare needs."

   Four recommendations were made that were to come into effect immediately:

a) More robust (i.e. stronger) and more comprehensive special guardian assessments and support plans with renewed emphasis on the child and special guardianship relationship.

b) Better preparation and training for Special Guardians.

c) A reduction in the use of Supervision Orders with Special Guardianship Orders.

d) Renewed emphasis on parental contact.

In addition the Working Group made **four aspirational recommendations**:-

i) Review of the fostering regulations.

ii) The possibility of interim Special Guardianship Orders.

iii) Further duties on Local Authorities to identify potential carers.

iv) The need for greater support for Special Guardians including a review of public funding for proposed Special Guardians.

The report expressed concerns over rushed assessments since the introduction of the 26-week time limit to complete care cases. It also sets out the options of testing out potential Special Guardianship Orders in situations where the child is not in a settled living arrangement with the potential Special Guardian.

6. In March 2021 the **Best Practice Guidance** provided some key themes which reinforce what had been set out in the June 2020 recommendations :

i) The assessment of a proposed Special Guardian should be thorough, comprehensive and evidence and experience informed.

ii) The support plan should be comprehensive and set out the support and services to be provided to the child and the prospective Special Guardian.

iii) Where there is little or no prior connection/relationship between the child and the prospective Special Guardian, it is very likely to be in the child's best interests to be cared for on an interim basis by the prospective Special Guardian in order to establish a meaningful relationship with the child.

iv) The Special Guardianship Support Plan should be based upon the lived experience of the child and the lived experience of the prospective Special Guardian

v) The Special Guardianship Support Plan should set out the **contact arrangements** between the child and parent(s) and should include: – The type of contact which is to take place – The frequency and duration of contact – Who is to be responsible for making the arrangements of contact – What practical arrangements need to be provided to facilitate contact – What professional support and assistance if any will be provided to the prospective Special Guardian.

vi) Save for cogent reasons, a supervision order should not be made alongside a Special Guardianship Order.

Local Authorities, practitioners and the courts are still getting to grips with all these proposals and practical changes.

CHAPTER FIFTEEN

PRACTICAL SUGGESTIONS WHEN ADVISING CLIENTS

Some practical suggestions when advising a grandparent client:

1. When meeting_with a grandparent for the first time, there needs to be a serious discussion about what is involved in seeking an order in respect of their grandchildren. You will need to emphasise that there will be a cost, both financially and emotionally. In most cases the financial cost of applying to the court for an order will be borne by the grandparent themselves. Legal aid is unlikely to be available and Local Authority financial help is often hard to achieve. Court applications may bring a grandparent into conflict with close relatives and friends which will be stressful and demanding. These are important factors to take into account before legal steps are taken to obtain a court order.

2. Is the matter resolvable by agreement? Could discussions within the family bring about a solution to the matters in hand? This may avoid unnecessary conflict and stress on both sides. Face to face meetings on an informal basis are usually more effective and can 'clear the air' on issues such as contact.

3. Will mediation help?

Mediation is the process by which families can negotiate about future arrangements for children with the help of a neutral third party. The mediator does not tell parties what to do, but can help the parties to reach their own agreements amicably, whilst trying to improve communication between them. There are several advantages to attending mediation such as:

- giving the parties more control over what decisions are made in relation to children, rather than applying to the courts;
- providing a less stressful way of dealing with sensitive matters;
- improving communication and helping parties sort out future arrangements;
- allowing arrangements to be reviewed and changed easier, so long as they are mutually agreed by both parties; and
- providing a quicker and cheaper way of resolving disputes.

4. Once a decision is made to take matters forward, does your client need permission to file an application? Is it possible that your client comes within the list of applicants who have automatic rights to apply for an order? Forms C2 or C100 are the commonly used forms of application depending on whether permission to apply is required.

5. If permission is required, does your grandparent client fit the **section 10(9)** criteria? Use the criteria set out **Re A (2015) All ER (D)** as a check list.

6. What type of order is your client seeking? Depending on what the grandparent is seeking to achieve these are likely to be: a Child Arrangements Order, Specific Issues Order, Prohibited Steps Order or Special Guardianship Order.

7. Assuming all these questions have been answered satisfactorily, you can proceed to complete the necessary forms, file them with the court to obtain a hearing date.

8. In the case of a variation or discharge of a SGO, has there been a *significant change* of circumstances. The focus has to be on the word 'significant' Each case will be different and will, of course, be judged on its merits. Special care should be taken not to raise the clients hopes unnecessarily. Any change should be clear and concrete. If there is a good and positive change an application to vary or discharge can be considered.

CHAPTER SIXTEEN

CONCLUSION

Despite much pressure on successive governments and politicians by organisations and individuals over the years, the rights of grandparents in the support of their grandchildren remains unchanged. There is still no special mention of grandparents in the current law, even including amendments to the Children Act 1989. Headlines in national newspapers appear to raise hopes; none of these have changed the position. Grandparents are seen as the first port of call when social workers in public proceedings look to place children from their parents' care. There can be little support on offer to them. In private proceedings grandparents are frequently expected to jump through a series of legal hoops before orders are made in their favour. Numerous lobby groups continue to campaign to bring about change on behalf of grandparents. For the time being the law remains unchanged. It is hoped that in due course grandparents will be recognised for who they are and that they will soon given the special position they deserve in English family law.

APPENDIX A

CHILDREN ACT 1989
PART III

SUPPORT FOR CHILDREN AND FAMILIES PROVIDED BY LOCAL AUTHORITIES IN ENGLAND

Ways in which looked after children are to be accommodated and maintained

(1) This section applies where a local authority are looking after a child ("C").

(2) The local authority must make arrangements for C to live with a person who falls within subsection (3) (but subject to subsection (4)).

(3) A person ("P") falls within this subsection if—

(a) P is a parent of C;

(b) P is not a parent of C but has parental responsibility for C; or

(c) in a case where C is in the care of the local authority and there was a child arrangements order in force with respect to C immediately before the care order was made, P was a person named in the child arrangements order as a person with whom C was to live.

(4) Subsection (2) does not require the local authority to make arrangements of the kind mentioned in that subsection if doing so—

(a) would not be consistent with C's welfare; or

(b) would not be reasonably practicable.

(5) If the local authority are unable to make arrangements under subsection (2), they must place C in the placement which is, in their opinion, the most appropriate placement available.

(6) In subsection (5) " placement " means—

(a) placement with an individual who is a relative, friend or other person connected with C and who is also a local authority foster parent;

(b) placement with a local authority foster parent who does not fall within paragraph (a);

(c) placement in a children's home in respect of which a person is registered under Part 2 of the Care Standards Act 2000; or

(d) subject to section 22D, placement in accordance with other arrangements which comply with any regulations made for the purposes of this section.

(7) In determining the most appropriate placement for C, the local authority must, subject to subsection (9B) and] the other provisions of this Part (in particular, to their duties under section 22)—

(a) give preference to a placement falling within paragraph (a) of subsection (6) over placements falling within the other paragraphs of that subsection;

(b) comply, so far as is reasonably practicable in all the circumstances of C's case, with the requirements of subsection (8); and

(c) comply with subsection (9) unless that is not reasonably practicable.

(8) The local authority must ensure that the placement is such that—

(a) it allows C to live near C's home;

(b) it does not disrupt C's education or training;

(c) if C has a sibling for whom the local authority are also providing accommodation, it enables C and the sibling to live together;

(d) if C is disabled, the accommodation provided is suitable to C's particular needs.

(9) The placement must be such that C is provided with accommodation within the local authority's area.

(9A) Subsection (9B) applies (subject to subsection (9C)) where the local authority...—

(a) are considering adoption for C, or

(b) are satisfied that C ought to be placed for adoption but are not authorised under section 19 of the Adoption and Children Act 2002 (placement with parental consent) or by virtue of section 21 of that Act (placement orders) to place C for adoption.

(9B) Where this subsection applies—

(a) subsections (7) to (9) do not apply to the local authority,

(b) the local authority must consider placing C with an individual within subsection (6)(a), and

(c) where the local authority decide that a placement with such an individual is not the most appropriate placement for C, the local authority must consider placing C with a local authority foster parent who has been approved as a prospective adopter.

(9C) Subsection (9B) does not apply where the local authority have applied for a placement order under section 21 of the Adoption and Children Act 2002 in respect of C and the application has been refused.

(10) The local authority may determine—

(a) the terms of any arrangements they make under subsection (2) in relation to C (including terms as to payment); and

(b) the terms on which they place C with a local authority foster parent (including terms as to payment but subject to any order made under section 49 of the Children Act 2004).

(11) The Secretary of State may make regulations for, and in connection with, the purposes of this section.

(12) For the meaning of "local authority foster parent" see section 105(1).

APPENDIX B

ADOPTION AND CHILDREN ACT 2002

Special guardianship

(1) After section 14 of the 1989 Act there is inserted—

"*Special guardianship*

14A Special guardianship orders

(1) A "special guardianship order" is an order appointing one or more individuals to be a child's "special guardian" (or special guardians).

(2) A special guardian—

(a) must be aged eighteen or over; and

(b) must not be a parent of the child in question,

and subsections (3) to (6) are to be read in that light.

(3) The court may make a special guardianship order with respect to any child on the application of an individual who—

(a) is entitled to make such an application with respect to the child; or

(b) has obtained the leave of the court to make the application,

or on the joint application of more than one such individual.

(4) Section 9(3) applies in relation to an application for leave to apply for a special guardianship order as it applies in relation to an application for leave to apply for a section 8 order.

(5) The individuals who are entitled to apply for a special guardianship order with respect to a child are—

(a) any guardian of the child;

(b) any individual in whose favour a residence order is in force with respect to the child;

(c) any individual listed in subsection (5)(b) or © of section 10 (as read with subsection (10) of that section);

(d) a local authority foster parent with whom the child has lived for a period of at least one year immediately preceding the application.

(6) The court may also make a special guardianship order with respect to a child in any family proceedings in which a question arises with respect to the welfare of the child if—

(a) an application for the order has been made by an individual who falls within subsection (3)(a) or (b) (or more than one such individual jointly); or

(b) the court considers that a special guardianship order should be made even though no such application has been made.

(7) No individual may make an application under subsection (3) or (6)(a) unless, before the beginning of the period of three months

ending with the date of the application, he has given written notice of his intention to make the application—

(a) if the child in question is being looked after by a local authority, to that local authority, or

(b) otherwise, to the local authority in whose area the individual is ordinarily resident.

(8) On receipt of such a notice, the local authority must investigate the matter and prepare a report for the court dealing with—

(a) the suitability of the applicant to be a special guardian;

(b) such matters (if any) as may be prescribed by the Secretary of State; and

(c) any other matter which the local authority consider to be relevant.

(9) The court may itself ask a local authority to conduct such an investigation and prepare such a report, and the local authority must do so.

(10) The local authority may make such arrangements as they see fit for any person to act on their behalf in connection with conducting an investigation or preparing a report referred to in subsection (8) or (9).

(11) The court may not make a special guardianship order unless it has received a report dealing with the matters referred to in subsection (8).

(12) Subsections (8) and (9) of section 10 apply in relation to special guardianship orders as they apply in relation to section 8 orders.

(13) This section is subject to section 29(5) and (6) of the Adoption and Children Act 2002.

14B Special guardianship orders: making

(1) Before making a special guardianship order, the court must consider whether, if the order were made—

(a) a contact order should also be made with respect to the child, and

(b) any section 8 order in force with respect to the child should be varied or discharged.

(2) On making a special guardianship order, the court may also—

(a) give leave for the child to be known by a new surname;

(b) grant the leave required by section 14C(3)(b), either generally or for specified purposes.

14C Special guardianship orders: effect

(1) The effect of a special guardianship order is that while the order remains in force—

(a) a special guardian appointed by the order has parental responsibility for the child in respect of whom it is made; and

(b) subject to any other order in force with respect to the child under this Act, a special guardian is entitled to exercise parental responsibility to the exclusion of any other person with parental responsibility for the child (apart from another special guardian).

(2) Subsection (1) does not affect—

(a) the operation of any enactment or rule of engineering which requires the consent of more than one person with parental responsibility in a matter affecting the child; or

(b) any rights which a parent of the child has in relation to the child's adoption or placement for adoption.

(3) While a special guardianship order is in force with respect to a child, no person may—

(a) cause the child to be known by a new surname; or

(b) remove him from the United Kingdom,

without either the written consent of every person who has parental responsibility for the child or the leave of the court.

(4) Subsection (3)(b) does not prevent the removal of a child, for a period of less than three months, by a special guardian of his.

(5) If the child with respect to whom a special guardianship order is in force dies, his special guardian must take reasonable steps to give notice of that fact to—

(a) each parent of the child with parental responsibility; and

(b) each guardian of the child,

but if the child has more than one special guardian, and one of them has taken such steps in relation to a particular parent or guardian, any other special guardian need not do so as respects that parent or guardian.

(6) This section is subject to section 29(7) of the Adoption and Children Act 2002.

14D Special guardianship orders: variation and discharge

(1) The court may vary or discharge a special guardianship order on the application of—

  (a) the special guardian (or any of them, if there are more than one);

  (b) any parent or guardian of the child concerned;

  (c) any individual in whose favour a residence order is in force with respect to the child;

  (d) any individual not falling within any of paragraphs (a) to © who has, or immediately before the making of the special guardianship order had, parental responsibility for the child;

  (e) the child himself; or

  (f) a local authority designated in a care order with respect to the child.

(2) In any family proceedings in which a question arises with respect to the welfare of a child with respect to whom a special guardianship order is in force, the court may also vary or discharge the special guardianship order if it considers that the order should be varied or discharged, even though no application has been made under subsection (1).

(3) The following must obtain the leave of the court before making an application under subsection (1)—

(a) the child;

(b) any parent or guardian of his;

(c) any step-parent of his who has acquired, and has not lost, parental responsibility for him by virtue of section 4A;

(d) any individual falling within subsection (1)(d) who immediately before the making of the special guardianship order had, but no longer has, parental responsibility for him.

(4) Where the person applying for leave to make an application under subsection (1) is the child, the court may only grant leave if it is satisfied that he has sufficient understanding to make the proposed application under subsection (1).

(5) The court may not grant leave to a person falling within subsection (3)(b)(c) or (d) unless it is satisfied that there has been a significant change in circumstances since the making of the special guardianship order.

14E Special guardianship orders: supplementary

(1) In proceedings in which any question of making, varying or discharging a special guardianship order arises, the court shall (in the light of any rules made by virtue of subsection (3))—

(a) draw up a timetable with a view to determining the question without delay; and

(b) give such directions as it considers appropriate for the purpose of ensuring, so far as is reasonably practicable, that the timetable is adhered to.

(2) Subsection (1) applies also in relation to proceedings in which any other question with respect to a special guardianship order arises.

(3) The power to make rules in subsection (2) of section 11 applies for the purposes of this section as it applies for the purposes of that.

(4) A special guardianship order, or an order varying one, may contain provisions which are to have effect for a specified period.

(5) Section 11(7) (apart from paragraph ©) applies in relation to special guardianship orders and orders varying them as it applies in relation to section 8 orders.

14F Special guardianship support services

(1) Each local authority must make arrangements for the provision within their area of special guardianship support services, which means—

(a) counselling, advice and information; and

(b) such other services as are prescribed,

in relation to special guardianship.

(2) The power to make regulations under subsection (1)(b) is to be exercised so as to secure that local authorities provide financial support.

(3) At the request of any of the following persons—

(a) a child with respect to whom a special guardianship order is in force;

(b) a special guardian;

(c) a parent;

(d) any other person who falls within a prescribed description,

a local authority may carry out an assessment of that person's needs for special guardianship support services (but, if the Secretary of State so provides in regulations, they must do so if he is a person of a prescribed description, or if his case falls within a prescribed description, or if both he and his case fall within prescribed descriptions).

(4) A local authority may, at the request of any other person, carry out an assessment of that person's needs for special guardianship support services.

(5) Where, as a result of an assessment, a local authority decide that a person has needs for special guardianship support services, they must then decide whether to provide any such services to that person.

(6) If—

(a) a local authority decide to provide any special guardianship support services to a person, and

(b) the circumstances fall within a prescribed description,

the local authority must prepare a plan in accordance with which special guardianship support services are to be provided to him, and keep the plan under review.

(7) The Secretary of State may by regulations make provision about assessments, preparing and reviewing plans, the provision of special guardianship support services in accordance with plans and reviewing the provision of special guardianship support services.

(8) The regulations may in particular make provision—

(a) about the type of assessment which is to be carried out, or the way in which an assessment is to be carried out;

(b) about the way in which a plan is to be prepared;

(c) about the way in which, and the time at which, a plan or the provision of special guardianship support services is to be reviewed;

(d) about the considerations to which a local authority are to have regard in carrying out an assessment or review or preparing a plan;

(e) as to the circumstances in which a local authority may provide special guardianship support services subject to conditions (including conditions as to payment for the support or the repayment of financial support);

(f) as to the consequences of conditions imposed by virtue of paragraph (e) not being met (including the recovery of any financial support provided);

(g) as to the circumstances in which this section may apply to a local authority in respect of persons who are outside that local authority's area;

(h) as to the circumstances in which a local authority may recover from another local authority the expenses of providing special guardianship support services to any person.

(9) A local authority may provide special guardianship support services (or any part of them) by securing their provision by—

(a) another local authority; or

(b) a person within a description prescribed in regulations of persons who may provide special guardianship support services,

and may also arrange with any such authority or person for that other authority or that person to carry out the local authority's functions in relation to assessments under this section.

(10) A local authority may carry out an assessment of the needs of any person for the purposes of this section at the same time as an assessment of his needs is made under any other provision of this Act or under any other enactment.

(11) Section 27 (co-operation between authorities) applies in relation to the exercise of functions of a local authority under this section as it applies in relation to the exercise of functions of a local authority under Part 3.

14G Special guardianship support services: representations

(1) Every local authority shall establish a procedure for considering representations (including complaints) made to them by any person to whom they may provide special guardianship support services about the discharge of their functions under section 14F in relation to him.

(2) Regulations may be made by the Secretary of State imposing time limits on the making of representations under subsection (1).

(3) In considering representations under subsection (1), a local authority shall comply with regulations (if any) made by the Secretary of State for the purposes of this subsection."

(2) The 1989 Act is amended as follows.

(3) In section 1 (welfare of the child), in subsection (4)(b), after "discharge" there is inserted "a special guardianship order or ".

(4) In section 5 (appointment of guardians)—

(a) in subsection (1)—

(i) in paragraph (b), for "or guardian" there is substituted " , guardian or special guardian ", and

(ii) at the end of paragraph (b) there is inserted "; or

(c) paragraph (b) does not apply, and the child's only or last surviving special guardian dies.",

(b) in subsection (4), at the end there is inserted "; and a special guardian of a child may appoint another individual to be the child's guardian in the event of his death", and

(c) in subsection (7), at the end of paragraph (b) there is inserted “or he was the child’s only (or last surviving) special guardian

APPENDIX C

PART 18 PROCEDURE FOR OTHER APPLICATIONS IN PROCEEDINGS

Contents of this Part

What an application notice must include	Rule 18.7
Service of a copy of an application notice	Rule 18.8
Applications which may be dealt with without a hearing	Rule 18.9
Service of application notice following court order where application made without notice	Rule 18.10
Application to set aside or vary order made without notice	Rule 18.11
Power of the court to proceed in the absence of a party	Rule 18.12
Dismissal of totally without merit applications	Rule 18.13

Types of application for which Part 18 procedure may be followed

18.1

(1) The Part 18 procedure is the procedure set out in this Part.

(2) An applicant may use the Part 18 procedure if the application is made –

(a) in the course of existing proceedings;

(b) to start proceedings except where some other Part of these rules prescribes the procedure to start proceedings; or

(c) in connection with proceedings which have been concluded.

(3) Paragraph (2) does not apply –

(a) to applications where any other rule in any other Part of these rules sets out the procedure for that type of application;

(b) if a practice direction provides that the Part 18 procedure may not be used in relation to the type of application in question.

Applications for permission to start proceedings

18.2

An application for permission to start proceedings must be made to the court where the proceedings will be started if permission is granted.

(Rule 5.4 makes general provision in relation to the court in which proceedings should be started.)

Respondents to applications under this Part

18.3

(1) The following persons are to be respondents to an application under this Part –

(a) where there are existing proceedings or the proceedings have been concluded –

   (i) the parties to those proceedings; and

   (ii) if the proceedings are proceedings under Part 11, the person who is the subject of those proceedings;

(b) where there are no existing proceedings –

   (i) if notice has been given under section 44 of the 2002 Act (notice of intention to adopt or apply for an order under section 84 of that Act), the local authority to whom notice has been given; and

   (ii) if an application is made for permission to apply for an order in proceedings, any person who will be a party to the proceedings brought if permission is granted; and

(c) any other person as the court may direct.

Application notice to be filed

18.4

(1) Subject to paragraph (2), the applicant must file an application notice.

(2) An applicant may make an application without filing an application notice if –

   (a) this is permitted by a rule or practice direction; or

(b) the court dispenses with the requirement for an application notice.

Notice of an application

18.5

(1) Subject to paragraph (2), a copy of the application notice must be served on –

(a) each respondent;

(b) in relation to proceedings under Part 11, the person who is, or, in the case of an application to start proceedings, it is intended will be, the subject of the proceedings; and

(c) in relation to proceedings under Parts 12 and 14, the children's guardian (if any).

(2) An application may be made without serving a copy of the application notice if this is permitted by –

(a) a rule;

(b) a practice direction; or

(c) the court.

(Rule 18.8 deals with service of a copy of the application notice.)

Time when an application is made

18.6

When an application must be made within a specified time, it is so made if the court receives the application notice within that time.

What an application notice must include

18.7

(1) An application notice must state –

(a) what order the applicant is seeking; and

(b) briefly, why the applicant is seeking the order.

(2) A draft of the order sought must be attached to the application notice.

(Part 17 requires an application notice to be verified by a statement of truth if the applicant wishes to rely on matters set out in his application as evidence.)

Service of a copy of an application notice

18.8

(1) Subject to rule 2.4, a copy of the application notice must be served in accordance with the provisions of Part 6 –

(a) as soon as practicable after it is filed; and

(b) in any event –

(i) where the application is for an order under rule 9.7 at least 14 days; and

(ii) in any other case, at least 7 days;

before the court is to deal with the application.

(2) The applicant must, when filing the application notice, file a copy of any written evidence in support.

(3) If a copy of an application notice is served by a court officer it must be accompanied by –

(a) a notice of the date and place where the application will be heard;

(b) a copy of any witness statement in support; and

(c) a copy of the draft order which the applicant has attached to the application.

(4) If –

(a) an application notice is served; but

(b) the period of notice is shorter than the period required by these rules or a practice direction,

the court may direct that, in the circumstances of the case, sufficient notice has been given and hear the application.

(5) This rule does not require written evidence –

(a) to be filed if it has already been filed; or

(b) to be served on a party on whom it has already been served.

Applications which may be dealt with without a hearing

18.9

(1) The court may deal with an application without a hearing if –

(a) the court does not consider that a hearing would be appropriate; or

(b) the parties agree as to the terms of the order sought or the parties agree that the court should dispose of the application without a hearing and the court does not consider that a hearing would be appropriate.

(2) Where –

(a) an application is made for permission to make an application in proceedings under the 1989 Act; and

(b) the court refuses the application without a hearing in accordance with paragraph (1)(a),

the court must, at the request of the applicant, re-list the application and fix a date for a hearing.

Service of application notice following court order where application made without notice

18.10

(1) This rule applies where the court has disposed of an application which it permitted to be made without service of a copy of the application notice.

(2) Where the court makes an order, whether granting or dismissing the application, a copy of the application notice and any evidence in support must unless the court orders otherwise, be served with the order on –

 (a) all the parties in proceedings; and

 (b) in relation to proceedings under Part 11, the person who is, or, in the case of an application to start proceedings, it is intended will be, the subject of the proceedings.

(3) The order must contain a statement of the right to make an application to set aside (GL) or vary the order under rule 18.11.

Application to set aside or vary order made without notice

18.11

(1) A person who was not served with a copy of the application notice before an order was made under rule 18.10 may apply to have the order set aside(GL) or varied.

(2) An application under this rule must be made within 7 days beginning with the date on which the order was served on the person making the application.

Power of the court to proceed in the absence of a party

18.12

(1) Where the applicant or any respondent fails to attend the hearing of an application, the court may proceed in the absence of that person.

(2) Where –

(a) the applicant or any respondent fails to attend the hearing of an application; and

(b) the court makes an order at the hearing,

the court may, on application or of its own initiative, re-list the application.

Dismissal of totally without merit applications

18.13

If the court dismisses an application (including an application for permission to appeal) and it considers that the application is totally without merit –

(a) the court's order must record that fact; and

(b) the court must at the same time consider whether it is appropriate to make a civil restraint order.

'A Practical Guide to Bad Character Evidence for Criminal Practitioners by Aparna Rao
'A Practical Guide to Extradition Law post-Brexit' by Myles Grandison et al
'A Practical Guide to Hoarding and Mental Health for Housing Lawyers' by Rachel Coyle
'A Practical Guide to Psychiatric Claims in Personal Injury – 2nd Edition' by Liam Ryan
'Stephens on Contractual Indemnities' by Richard Stephens
'A Practical Guide to the EU Succession Regulation' by Richard Frimston
'A Practical Guide to Solicitor and Client Costs – 2nd Edition' by Robin Dunne
'Constructive Dismissal – Practice Pointers and Principles' by Benjimin Burgher
'A Practical Guide to Religion and Belief Discrimination Claims in the Workplace' by Kashif Ali
'A Practical Guide to the Law of Medical Treatment Decisions' by Ben Troke
'Fundamental Dishonesty and QOCS in Personal Injury Proceedings: Law and Practice' by Jake Rowley
'A Practical Guide to the Law in Relation to School Exclusions' by Charlotte Hadfield & Alice de Coverley
'A Practical Guide to Divorce for the Silver Separators' by Karin Walker
'The Right to be Forgotten – The Law and Practical Issues' by Melissa Stock
'A Practical Guide to Planning Law and Rights of Way in National Parks, the Broads and AONBs' by James Maurici QC, James Neill et al
'A Practical Guide to Election Law' by Tom Tabori
'A Practical Guide to the Law in Relation to Surrogacy' by Andrew Powell
'A Practical Guide to Claims Arising from Fatal Accidents – 2nd Edition' by James Patience
'A Practical Guide to the Ownership of Employee Inventions – From Entitlement to Compensation' by James Tumbridge & Ashley Roughton
'A Practical Guide to Asbestos Claims' by Jonathan Owen & Gareth McAloon
'A Practical Guide to Stamp Duty Land Tax in England and Northern Ireland' by Suzanne O'Hara
'A Practical Guide to the Law of Farming Partnerships' by Philip Whitcomb
'Covid-19, Homeworking and the Law – The Essential Guide to Employment and GDPR Issues' by Forbes Solicitors
'Covid-19 and Criminal Law – The Essential Guide' by Ramya Nagesh

'Covid-19 and Family Law in England and Wales – The Essential Guide' by Safda Mahmood

'A Practical Guide to the Law of Unlawful Eviction and Harassment – 2nd Edition' by Stephanie Lovegrove

'Covid-19, Brexit and the Law of Commercial Leases – The Essential Guide' by Mark Shelton

'A Practical Guide to Costs in Personal Injury Claims – 2nd Edition' by Matthew Hoe

'A Practical Guide to the General Data Protection Regulation (GDPR) – 2nd Edition' by Keith Markham

'Ellis on Credit Hire – Sixth Edition' by Aidan Ellis & Tim Kevan

'A Practical Guide to Working with Litigants in Person and McKenzie Friends in Family Cases' by Stuart Barlow

'Protecting Unregistered Brands: A Practical Guide to the Law of Passing Off' by Lorna Brazell

'A Practical Guide to Secondary Liability and Joint Enterprise Post-Jogee' by Joanne Cecil & James Mehigan

'A Practical Guide to the Pre-Action RTA Claims Protocol for Personal Injury Lawyers' by Antonia Ford

'A Practical Guide to Neighbour Disputes and the Law' by Alexander Walsh

'A Practical Guide to Forfeiture of Leases' by Mark Shelton

'A Practical Guide to Coercive Control for Legal Practitioners and Victims' by Rachel Horman

'A Practical Guide to Rights Over Airspace and Subsoil' by Daniel Gatty

'Tackling Disclosure in the Criminal Courts – A Practitioner's Guide' by Narita Bahra QC & Don Ramble

'A Practical Guide to the Law of Driverless Cars – Second Edition' by Alex Glassbrook, Emma Northey & Scarlett Milligan

'A Practical Guide to TOLATA Claims' by Greg Williams

'A Practical Guide to Elderly Law – 2nd Edition' by Justin Patten

'A Practical Guide to Responding to Housing Disrepair and Unfitness Claims' by Iain Wightwick

'A Practical Guide to the Construction and Rectification of Wills and Trust Instruments' by Edward Hewitt

'A Practical Guide to the Law of Bullying and Harassment in the Workplace' by Philip Hyland

'How to Be a Freelance Solicitor: A Practical Guide to the SRA-Regulated Freelance Solicitor Model' by Paul Bennett
'A Practical Guide to Prison Injury Claims' by Malcolm Johnson
'A Practical Guide to the Small Claims Track - 2nd Edition' by Dominic Bright
'A Practical Guide to Advising Clients at the Police Station' by Colin Stephen McKeown-Beaumont
'A Practical Guide to Antisocial Behaviour Injunctions' by Iain Wightwick
'Practical Mediation: A Guide for Mediators, Advocates, Advisers, Lawyers, and Students in Civil, Commercial, Business, Property, Workplace, and Employment Cases' by Jonathan Dingle with John Sephton
'The Mini-Pupillage Workbook' by David Boyle
'A Practical Guide to Crofting Law' by Brian Inkster
'A Practical Guide to Spousal Maintenance' by Liz Cowell
'A Practical Guide to the Law of Domain Names and Cybersquatting' by Andrew Clemson
'A Practical Guide to the Law of Gender Pay Gap Reporting' by Harini Iyengar
'NHS Whistleblowing and the Law' by Joseph England
'Employment Law and the Gig Economy' by Nigel Mackay & Annie Powell
'A Practical Guide to Noise Induced Hearing Loss (NIHL) Claims' by Andrew Mckie, Ian Skeate, Gareth McAloon
'An Introduction to Beauty Negligence Claims – A Practical Guide for the Personal Injury Practitioner' by Greg Almond
'Intercompany Agreements for Transfer Pricing Compliance' by Paul Sutton
'Zen and the Art of Mediation' by Martin Plowman
'A Practical Guide to the SRA Principles, Individual and Law Firm Codes of Conduct 2019 – What Every Law Firm Needs to Know' by Paul Bennett
'A Practical Guide to Adoption for Family Lawyers' by Graham Pegg
'A Practical Guide to Industrial Disease Claims' by Andrew Mckie & Ian Skeate
'A Practical Guide to Redundancy' by Philip Hyland
'A Practical Guide to Vicarious Liability' by Mariel Irvine
'A Practical Guide to Applications for Landlord's Consent and Variation of Leases' by Mark Shelton
'A Practical Guide to Relief from Sanctions Post-Mitchell and Denton' by Peter Causton

'A Practical Guide to Equity Release for Advisors' by Paul Sams
'A Practical Guide to Financial Services Claims' by Chris Hegarty
'The Law of Houses in Multiple Occupation: A Practical Guide to HMO Proceedings' by Julian Hunt
'Occupiers, Highways and Defective Premises Claims: A Practical Guide Post-Jackson – 2nd Edition' by Andrew Mckie
'A Practical Guide to Financial Ombudsman Service Claims' by Adam Temple & Robert Scrivenor
'A Practical Guide to Advising Schools on Employment Law' by Jonathan Holden
'A Practical Guide to Running Housing Disrepair and Cavity Wall Claims: 2nd Edition' by Andrew Mckie & Ian Skeate
'A Practical Guide to Holiday Sickness Claims – 2nd Edition' by Andrew Mckie & Ian Skeate
'Arguments and Tactics for Personal Injury and Clinical Negligence Claims' by Dorian Williams
'A Practical Guide to Drone Law' by Rufus Ballaster, Andrew Firman, Eleanor Clot
'A Practical Guide to Compliance for Personal Injury Firms Working With Claims Management Companies' by Paul Bennett
'RTA Allegations of Fraud in a Post-Jackson Era: The Handbook – 2nd Edition' by Andrew Mckie
'RTA Personal Injury Claims: A Practical Guide Post-Jackson' by Andrew Mckie
'On Experts: CPR35 for Lawyers and Experts' by David Boyle
'An Introduction to Personal Injury Law' by David Boyle

www.ingramcontent.com/pod-product-compliance
Lightning Source LLC
LaVergne TN
LVHW022059200926
848481LV00003B/995
* 9 7 8 1 9 1 4 6 0 8 9 1 9 *